Gloria P-U

The Hidden Scarlet Sin

by
Victoria Milstead

DORRANCE PUBLISHING CO., INC.
PITTSBURGH, PENNSYLVANIA 15222

ISBN # 0-8059-3281-X
Printed in the United States of America

First Printing

I dedicate this book
to all those who
have been victims of the
sexual revolution.

I

The sky was an azure blue, the new, young leaves on the trees were a pale shade of green, and the flowers on the trees were a lovely shade of pink and white. It was April, her favorite month of the year, but Angela Miriam Sutton noticed none of it. She usually was uplifted by the beauty of the spring season, but this year her heart was too heavy to enjoy the loveliness that the budding of the spring always brought. As she rode her bicycle down Elmwood past the church building where she and her parents attended services, she tried not to notice the parsonage where her best friend, Cheryl Barrett, lived with her brother, Ted, and their parents, Dr. and Mrs. Barrett. She knew that she had not seen much of Cheryl recently, and she hoped that Cheryl was still her very best friend. Angela felt embarrassed and too ashamed to even speak to Cheryl, much less go places with her. Today she promised Cheryl she would meet her at McDonald's down on Oak Street. In some way she was eager to meet Cheryl this time. Angela wanted to tell her friend about the date she had with Rob for the dance tonight at school. Angela was glad her parents let her go with the boy although she could not "car date" as she was only fourteen. She hoped this event would push all the worries she had to the back of her mind for the time being.

Angela parked her bike in the driveway at the McDonald's on Oak and went inside where Cheryl and another girl, Wendy Barton, were waiting for her. Cheryl had ordered milkshakes for the three of them, and she was relieved that Angela had finally arrived.

"I was just about to give up on you, Angela," she complained.

"Sorry," Angela explained, "but I had to finish my Saturday morning chores."

She sat and sipped her chocolate milkshake while Wendy and Cheryl conversed about the dance that evening. They were all being escorted by boys in the ninth grade although Angela was in the eighth grade. Cheryl and Wendy were one year older than she was. In the nearby seat, some kids a year or two older than Angela and her friends were talking and giggling over some tabloids they were reading. Suddenly, one of the boys said something about a story in one of the tabloids about a man of the cloth who had been caught in a sex scandal. The youth seemed to think the report was funny, and he showed the article around to the other boys and girls seated near him.

Cheryl stood up and went over to the youngster and snatched the tabloid from him. "I don't think that is one bit funny!" she exclaimed.

"I mean no offense, preacher's kid," the boy said. "Fact is, this has nothing to do with you or your dad. So why get uptight?"

"I just don't think it is something to laugh about. That's all," Cheryl explained. "I don't mean to be preachy or anything."

"Come on, Cheryl." Wendy led her friend back to their seat. "Let them be."

"It was immature of them to laugh at that story, don't you think, Angela?" Cheryl leaned over to talk to Angela, but her friend was not there in her seat. She had gotten up and vanished. Cheryl stood up and noticed Angela peddling away down Oak Street on her bike.

"I wonder why she left, Wendy," Cheryl mused. "She only half finished her milkshake. Oh, well, she has been acting strange lately. I don't know what is bugging her."

❄

Florence Sutton was working in her yard cutting freshly bloomed lilac blossoms from their stems to put in a vase to decorate the living room. She was humming to herself a song she had learned years ago. Too bad young people today don't sing good songs like this today, she reflected. They are too interested in hard rock, it seems. Angela was her and Mark's youngest child, born when their two sons and older daughter were into their teens. She had been in her early forties when Angela was born, so there was quite an age difference between parents and child. They were not overprotective of her, and they were actually glad to permit her to go out on her first date tonight although they had both been older when they had their first dates.

Florence had just finished cutting the last stem of lilac when a van drove up. She recognized the van immediately—it was the Reverend Dr. Ronald Barrett, the senior minister of their church. I wonder what he wants, Florence thought to herself. He probably just wants to visit, although he usually comes when he has some business to discuss.

"Good morning, Florence," Dr. Barrett greeted her. "Is Mark home this morning? I have something very important to discuss with both of you."

"Oh, yes, Mark is home," Florence replied. "I was just going to put these lilacs in a vase. Come in, won't you, Dr. Barrett."

Florence led Dr. Barrett into the living room and called for her husband. Then she went into the kitchen to fetch a vase, fill it with water, and place the lilacs in it. When she had completed this task, she took the flower-filled vase into the living room where Mark and Dr. Barrett were, and set the vase on the coffee table.

Dr. Ronald Theodore Barrett was forty-four years of age, with hazel eyes and dark hair which was beginning to turn gray at the temples. He was slightly near-sighted and wore wire-rimmed eyeglasses. His appearance was often described as handsome but dignified. "Dignified" was most often the description given to him by Mrs. Audrey Keller, a sexagenarian who was a member of his congregation and also a good friend of the Suttons. Mrs. Keller used to babysit for Angela when the girl was little while both her parents worked. That Dr. Barrett had something urgent to discuss with the Suttons was apparent.

"My daughter, Cheryl, just told my wife and me about Angela's so-called date for tonight," he began, with a very disapproving tone in his voice.

"That's right," Mark explained, "we're glad to say that Angela has her first date tonight for the junior high school dance."

"Doesn't it occur to you," Dr. Barrett said, "that Angela is too young to date?"

Too young? The Suttons pondered this presumptuous remark made by their pastor. True, they did not begin dating until Florence was fifteen and Mark was sixteen. But that was nearly forty years ago, and young people seemed to be growing up earlier these days.

"But we have given her our permission, Dr. Barrett," Florence stated. "We don't think we're letting her grow up too soon."

"All the same, Angela is too young to go out on a date." It seemed to really disturb Dr. Barrett that Angela Sutton was going out on a date with a boy. He seemed even angry and resentful, if that was what one could call it.

"Girls have to grow up some time," Florence remarked. "Angela is actually mature for her age physically. So she really looks older than she is."

"Growing up is what she has been doing, all right," Mark commented. "She has to get out and start meeting boys."

"She won't mature emotionally unless she is allowed to be normal," said Florence. "I wonder if you will miss all those trips you have been taking with her, Dr. Barrett. She won't be able to grow up if you keep climbing trees and going bird-watching with her."

Dr. Barrett flinched, and a strange look came over his handsome face. He looked, the Suttons thought, almost frightened. That, of course, was absurd. What was there for him to be afraid of? They were fully aware that Dr. Barrett had been taking Angela and Cheryl on outings in the woods to do some bird-watching and picnicking. There was nothing unusual about that, two friends together with the father of one of them. The Suttons were used to other adults taking Angela places and entertaining her. This had been going on since she was four years old when Florence started to work full time.

Dr. Barrett rose to leave. "I only hope you know what you're doing. That child needs to grow up some more before she starts to—er—date."

Florence saw him to the door, asking him about his wife and children. They were doing fine, thank you. The Suttons bade Dr. Barrett goodbye saying they would see him the next day at the Sunday morning service.

Angela was riding her bicycle into her yard as Dr. Barrett started to board his van. He greeted her: "Hello, Angel, how are you this bright spring morning?"

Angela bowed her head as she did not want her eyes to meet his. She felt a blush come over her face. "I'm fine, Dr. Barrett. Did you come to see me, if you know what I mean. But my parents are home, you see, so...," she broke off, flustered.

"I came to see your parents, Angel," her pastor explained. "So I'll see you tomorrow morning. OK? Goodbye, now." He climbed into the van and drove away.

❄

That evening Angela dressed for the dance, and she looked forward to her very first date. She donned the sky-blue silk dress her mother had bought for her, thinking that it must be the most beautiful dress in the world. As she buttoned up the back, she reflected on how the blue of the dress brought out the blue of her eyes. Her family always told her how much a beauty she was. Her blue eyes were her mother's as was her white skin, but her hair was jet black like her father's. Her older sister, Hannah Rose, had brown hair like their mother. Angela missed her sister who was now married, had two small children, and a full-time job. A real "super-mom" Hannah was.

When she was finished dressing, Angela regarded herself in the full-length mirror. The light blue dress had long sleeves and a white lace collar. She put on a heart-shaped pendant to accentuate the collar. Perfect, she thought. She turned sideways and looked at herself in the mirror. She had a full, voluptuous figure, so curvy that she looked eighteen instead of fourteen. Angela used to admire her figure and her beauty, but now she felt that all this lushness had caused the trouble. I won't think about that now, she thought. I don't want him or anything else to upset this evening. I am determined to enjoy myself. She retrieved her white dress-up jacket from her closet and went downstairs.

When Angela reached the bottom of the stairway, both her parents were waiting for her. Florence commented on how lovely her daughter looked, but Mark only glanced at her and looked away as if afraid to really look at her. Angela paid no attention to this, however; she was by now accustomed to this type of treatment from her father.

Mark drove Angela to first pick up her date, Rob McAlester, and then they drove to the dance. Mark would take them back home when the party was over.

Angela tried to enjoy herself as she vowed she would. She danced most of the numbers with Rob, although he permitted her to dance with some other boys. After she had been there for nearly an hour, Angela heard one of the songs being played. It was "Angel of the Morning" sung by Juice Newton. Listening to the lyrics, Angela felt they hit very close to home, and she could hardly dance, so upsetting were these words. After this number, a record was played that required slow dancing with the partners holding each other close. Rob took Angela into his arms and danced with her. But Angela suddenly could not take this closeness. Blinded by emotional pain, she pushed herself away and ran out of the room.

Later that evening, as Angela waited with Rob for her dad to pick them up, she apologized for her rude behavior. Rob said it was nothing and brought her a cup of punch.

"Would you like to go to a movie with me next Friday night, Angela?" Rob asked her.

"I don't know," Angela replied. "What kind of movie? My folks think a lot of movies are unsuitable nowadays."

"Don't worry. It's rated 'PG' so it won't have anything too bad in it, I hope."

"All right. I'll talk to my dad when he takes me home. OK?"

"OK."

After they had dropped Rob off at his house, Angela asked her father about the next date with Rob on the following Friday. Mark, after hearing what the movie was about, gave his permission for Angela to go.

"Oh, thanks, Dad," Angela exclaimed, giving him a hug from which Mark immediately backed away. Angela apologized, wishing she would not have to apologize.

"So you really enjoyed yourself," Mark said.

"Yeah, I did. I never thought a dance could really be so much fun." Angela did not tell him about the scary feeling she had experienced out on the dance floor, but then she could not actually tell anyone at all.

When they arrived home, Angela went straight up to bed. She felt tired tonight. She would have a good night's rest for once. The only thing bothering her was the fact that the next day was Sunday, meaning she would have to go to Sunday School and then to church where he would be.

❊

When Dr. Barrett came home from picking up Cheryl at the school dance, he figured his wife, Joan, would already be in bed. He just hoped she would not be asleep right away. As he tiptoed into their bedroom, he noticed that the lamp on Joan's side of the bed was on. Joan was still awake sitting up reading an issue of *Christianity Today.* Her husband slipped into the bathroom to don his pajamas. Joan went on reading as if she didn't know he was there. When Ron emerged from the bathroom, he commented on Cheryl's fun evening at the dance. But he also said that she was now old enough to date whereas Angela Sutton was too young. Why did he talk so much about Angela, Joan wondered. After Ron crawled into bed, Joan put down her magazine, reached over and turned off the light. She knew she would have a very restful night, Ron would not bother her. Strange I should think of it as "bothering," she reflected. It had been a long time since they had last made love. Once upon a time, before the children were born, and for a while right after that, she used to look forward to their lovemaking sessions. After Ted's birth, twelve years ago, was when all the conflict began. I won't think about that now, she thought. If I do then I won't be able to sleep. She closed her eyes and tried to think of quiet, peaceful meadows....

❄

Angela awoke to the scent of frying bacon and rolls baking in the oven. Sunday breakfast was always the best, except for Saturday breakfast which was usually either pancakes or waffles. But Sundays the family always had scrambled eggs with bacon, rolls, and sausage. Strange, she had not had any nightmares last night. She usually woke up at least once every night in a cold sweat. And she could never remember what she had dreamed. But she would know for certain the dreams had been bad from the way her heart would be pounding and the stickiness of her palms. She arose, went to the bathroom, washed her face, and donned her bathrobe. She slowly descended the stairs and went into the kitchen to have breakfast with her parents. It was going to be another sunny, mild day, she thought looking out the kitchen window. After breakfast, Angela helped her mother clean off the table and wash the dishes.

When she was ready for Sunday School and church, dressed in her light pink dress and wearing a hat bedecked with matching pink flowers, Angela joined her parents in the hall downstairs. It was such a lovely morning that Mark and Florence suggested that they walk to the church building as it was only two blocks away. Angela agreed, hoping that the walk would cheer her up although she doubted it. The street was lined with budding trees and shrubbery—forsythia bushes, pink flowering crabtrees, dogwoods, apple trees, and peach trees. They were each and every one breathtakingly beautiful, a sign that spring was finally here. The morning sky was a deep blue, and it went perfectly with the greening, flowering scenery.

The church had two Sunday morning worship services, one at 9:30 when Sunday School was in session, and one at 11:00 when most of the adults attended. Dr. Barrett and the associate pastor, the Reverend Schiller, often took turns preaching and acting as liturgist. Angela at one time had sung in the youth choir, but now she attended Sunday School at 9:30 and the worship service at 11:00 with her parents as well as the junior high youth group which met every other Sunday evening.

Angela went to her class while her parents left her for theirs. Angela had the opportunity to play the piano for her class this morning. She was hoping that she could suggest a song. When the time came, she named "The Old Rugged Cross," and played with gusto as she tried to put her heart into her playing. When this was finished, the class said a prayer and then proceeded with the lesson, which was on the story of Jesus calming the waters for the disciples while they were in a boat on the Sea of Galilee. Angela anxiously watched the clock as it ticked the time away, knowing that soon the class would end and then it would be time to go downstairs into the sanctuary for the worship service.

When the bell rang to announce the end of Sunday School, the class said a closing prayer and then departed. Angela went downstairs, passing the fellowship hall, and through the door leading to the front of the sanctuary. She went this way hoping she would not meet up with Dr. Barrett who would naturally be at the front door with Reverend Schiller shaking hands and saying good morning to the people who had attended the 9:30 service. But it was to no avail because when she passed through the door, he was there—waiting for her, so it seemed.

"Good morning, Angela," he greeted her. "Surely you remember your youth group meeting for tonight."

"Good morning, Dr. Barrett. I did not forget youth group."

"I'll bring you home afterward. Your parents will think that you spent the extra time with Cheryl or one of your other friends, if you know what I mean."

Angela blushed furiously. She knew what he meant! And on a Sunday, too! How could he, standing there wearing his black robe and white mantel suggest it to her? Maybe I could make some excuse, she plotted to herself. No, that wouldn't be right. Mom and Dad will wonder why I don't want to attend youth group.

"You don't have to bother taking me home, Dr. Barrett," was all she could say. "I can walk."

"No, I insist. It gets dark by the time group ends, and I wouldn't want you to walk home in the dark."

"All right."

What hypocrites we are, Angela thought. We are living double lives, he and I. How long can this go on? I just wish I had the nerve to end it!

II

As Dr. Barrett went into the fellowship hall to meet with those leaving Sunday School, Angela went to her parents' favorite pew. She sat huddled up and blinked to keep back the tears. Her father came up and sat down beside her and handed her a church bulletin while her mother talked with Mrs. Keller, who usually sat with them. Soon the worship service began, and Angel did not look up as Dr. Barrett and Reverend Schiller walked down the aisle. The congregation soon rose to sing the processional hymn, "Onward Christian Soldiers." Dr. Barrett's sermon that morning was based on John 14:1-14:

> "Do not let your hearts be troubled. Trust in God; trust also in me. In my Father's house are many rooms; if it were not so, I would have told you. I am going there to prepare a place for you. And if I go and prepare a place for you, I will come back and take you to be with me that you also may be where I am. You know the way to the place where I am going." Thomas said to him, "Lord, we don't know where you are going, so how can we know the way?" Jesus answered, "I am the way and the truth and the life. No one comes to the Father except through me. If you really knew me, you would know my Father as well. From now on, you do know him and have seen him." Philip said, "Lord, show us the Father and that will be enough for us." Jesus answered: "Don't you know me, Philip, even after I have been among you such a long time? Anyone who has seen me has seen the Father. How can you say, 'Show us the Father'? Don't you believe that I am in the Father, and that the Father is in me? The words I say to you are not just my own. Rather, it is the Father, living in me, who is doing his work. Believe me when I say that I am in the Father and the Father is in me; or at least believe on the evidence of the miracles themselves. I tell you the truth, anyone who has faith in me will do what I have been doing. He will do even greater things than these, because I am going to the Father. And I will do whatever you ask in my name, so that the Son may bring glory to the Father. You may ask me for anything in my name, and I will do it."

After listening to the minister read this passage from the scriptures, Angela could barely pay attention. She wondered how he could do this, considering what went on at other times. I won't think about that, I must put such thoughts out of my mind, she said to herself.

When the service was finished, and the benediction had been said, Angela went with her parents and Mrs. Keller out the front door. Angela hoped that she could avoid meeting Dr. Barrett, but she could not. Once again he reminded her about the junior high youth group meeting that night and how he would bring her home. Angela then hurried away so quickly that she did not even say goodbye to Mrs. Keller, who was a good friend of hers as well as her parents. Mark and Florence eventually caught up with their daughter and Florence indignantly asked Angela why she had been so rude.

"I'm sorry, Mom," Angela apologized. "I just want to get home, I guess."

"What did the minister say to you just now, honey?" Florence asked.

"Oh, it was nothing. He just reminded me about my youth group meeting this evening." Angela ran off, unable to hold back the tears. When she arrived home, however, her eyes were dried. She did not want her folks to know how upset she was because then they would start asking questions.

Angela fixed herself a snack lunch while her parents sat down in front of the television to watch a Kansas City Royals baseball game. She did not care too much for sports, but her parents were Royals fans so they enjoyed the games. She fetched her bicycle from the garage and rode around the neighborhood hoping that she would be able to keep her mind off the coming evening. She tried to concentrate on the blooming spring, the robins, meadowlarks, and bluebirds who had come back north after spending the winter in the south. But this only reminded her of the bird-watching excursions with Dr. Barrett, so she tried to think about something else like her schoolwork. Angela had once been a straight-A student, but this year she was making Cs and Ds. Her parents were very concerned about this, and more than a few times the school counselor had called them in to talk with her. Angela loved her mother and father, of course, and she did not want to disappoint them by doing schoolwork that was beneath her capability. I'll have to try harder, she reflected, but, darn it, it seems I can't!

When she returned home, Angela put her bike back in the garage. She then went upstairs to attempt studying. However, she was unable to concentrate, as always these days, so she went over to her bed and lay down in an effort to take a nap. She was not sure how much time had passed when her dad knocked on the door and told her it was time for Sunday dinner. It was her favorite—fried chicken.

After dinner Angela went upstairs to get ready for her youth group meeting. She donned lavender slacks, a white blouse sprigged with lilacs, and a light purple sweater. She brushed her shoulder-length hair and tied back a part with a lavender ribbon. Then she went downstairs.

"I think I'll walk to the meeting, Mom and Dad," she told her parents. "I plan to spend the rest of the evening with friends, OK?"

"That's fine, dear," replied Florence, "just as long as we know where you are and that you get home safely."

Angela kissed her folks goodbye and started off to the church where the meeting was to be held in the fellowship hall. A good thing about springtime and daylight savings was that it provided more light in the evening, and one could take evening walks.

Throughout the meeting, Angela sat nervously and anxiously knowing what was to come afterward. She kept thinking and hoping that Dr. Barrett would forget or maybe change his mind. But toward the end of the group meeting, he showed up after all. Her heart sank, and she looked away from him as she did not want to face him. Finally, after a word of prayer, the meeting broke up and he approached her.

"It is time to go, Angela," he said. "Did you remember you-know-what?"

"Yes, I remembered." Angela glanced around the room, hoping fervently that Cheryl or one of the other kids would stop them. But it was not to be.

❈

An hour or so later, Dr. Barrett drove up in front of the Sutton house to let Angela off. But before she could disembark, he spoke to her severely: "Remember, not a word of this to anyone. You know very well that this is our little secret."

"I know, Dr. Barrett, not a word," Angela replied. But because she could bear it no more, she burst out, "Why do we keep doing this? It is wrong, I know it! If anyone should find out, we would be in serious trouble, just like you once said!"

Dr. Barrett spoke even more sharply to her: "No one will ever find out because you promised not to breathe a word to anyone. And it is our little secret, like I just now said, isn't it?"

"I wish I had never promised anything."

"Oh, and don't forget Friday night is our bowling night. Your parents think that you are going with friends, don't they?"

"Yes, but I have a date with Rob McAlester this coming Friday night! I didn't tell you."

"You forgot our bowling night, didn't you?"

"It's not that. It's just that I want to go to a movie with Rob, that's all. I have to start dating soon, anyway."

"Not right now. You're too young, and I don't want you to go out with anyone."

Angela was aghast at this. "What right do you have to tell me I can't go out on a date! You're not my father!"

"I am still in a position of authority to you."

"But there is still a higher authority! Considering what we're doing, what if I took it in mind to write the bishop about it?"

Dr. Barrett gripped his hand on Angela's shoulder so hard it hurt. "I told you that you are not to tell anyone—not by word of mouth or by letter! Do you understand?"

Angela winced with both emotional and physical pain. "Yes, sir. Not a word!"

"Here, you must not forget these."

Angela left the van and went up the sidewalk as the van drove off. She tried hard to keep back the tears, but they spilled over and ran down her cheeks. When she entered the house, her father was in the living room watching the news. He asked her if she had a good time at the meeting and with her friends, as he figured that she had spent time with her girlfriends, after the youth group meeting. Angela only nodded and hurried up the stairs. She went into the bathroom, got undressed and took a hot shower. She could not help it, but she felt unclean—as if she could never be clean again. When she was finished with her shower and dressed in her nightgown, she sat at her vanity and brushed her hair. Florence came in and sat down on her daughter's bed.

"What's wrong, honey?" she asked. "Your dad says you were crying when you came in."

"It's nothing, Mom," Angela responded.

"It can't be nothing. Did you have a fight with one of your friends? Did you argue with Cheryl?"

"No, I didn't fight with Cheryl. I had an argument with her dad. He drove me home."

"An argument? With the minister? Angela Sutton, you know you aren't supposed to argue or talk back to adults!"

"But, Mom, he objects to my going out with Rob this Friday night! And I already have your permission and Dad's."

"That's true. Well, your father and I will have a talk with Dr. Barrett. He may be our minister, but that doesn't give him the right to rule our lives."

When Angela finished brushing her hair, she went to brush her teeth and get into bed. Florence tucked her in and, for once, Angela did not protest by saying that she was too big to have her mother tuck her into bed.

Angela slept restlessly that night. She had a bad dream in which she saw herself wearing a white dress. But when she looked into the mirror, she saw that the dress was not white but a bright scarlet. In another dream, she looked into a mirror and beheld her reflection. She was diseased with a terrible kind of leprosy. She awoke with a cry.

What a nightmare! she thought. She knelt down by her bed and prayed a simple prayer: "Dearest Jesus, help me with this. If You can hear me then help me. Rescue me from this. As You cleansed the lepers, please cleanse me from this spiritual disease. Help me! Amen."

The morning dawned fair and bright for the third straight day in a row. There was more humidity, however, promising rain within twenty-four hours. Angela dressed and went down to breakfast. She found her parents seated around the breakfast table where Florence was serving coffee. Angela took her seat and commenced eating her breakfast. She kept thinking, what if he calls me this afternoon after school when I am home alone. Or maybe he will call on me in person. That's worse! Suddenly she burst out: "Mom, why can't you stay home with me instead of working? I mean, since you don't really have to work now, you can stay here with me. Not all mothers work."

Both Florence and Mark were taken aback by this sudden outburst of Angela's. True, Florence originally began working ten years earlier in the days of double-digit inflation. During that time, Angela had spent her days with the Kellers. After she started school, she would go to the Kellers' after school where she would watch reruns of "Gilligan's Island," "The Beverly Hillbillies," and "Little House on the Prairie." When Angela was twelve, Mr. Keller died, and Mrs. Keller still invited Angela over after school. Angela still went to Mrs. Keller's, but usually she preferred to go home and stay alone until her parents returned. Her mother often had her help prepare supper so that Florence could finish it when she came home. Angela had indeed become a modern "latch-key kid."

"Now, Angela," Mark rebuked his daughter, "your mother works hard, and she is proud of her work. Look at Hannah. She has two children and she works full-time at a job harder than your mother's."

Angela felt ashamed but hurt. She knew that both of Hannah's children were placed in a day care center all day. Her niece was four and her nephew was eighteen months. She felt sorry for them having to be away from their mother all day at such young ages. At least, she reflected, Mom was home with me when I was eighteen months old.

"I'm sorry, Mom and Dad," she apologized, "I guess I just spoke without thinking."

When Angela finished her breakfast, she went upstairs to fetch her school books. When she came back downstairs, Mark offered to drive her to school on his way to work.

"Thanks, Dad. But you don't have to. I can walk."

"Sure? Well, OK. Bye now, see you at suppertime."

Florence stopped her daughter as Angela was about to step out the door. "Oh, hon, I want you to talk with your guidance counselor today. You remember how she called us in the other day. It seems you're not doing quite as well this year as you usually do."

"I will, Mom."

"Angela, are you sure there isn't something bothering you?"

"No, Mom, I'm all right."

As Angela walked to school, her father drove up offering once more to give her a lift. This time she accepted. It would not hurt to be a little early anyway.

❄

Angela sat in the office of Mrs. Bergmeier, the girls' guidance counselor. She took her mother's advice and came to this office during fifth period when she had study hall. Mrs. Bergmeier was discussing Angela's grades so far this year.

"I'm surprised, Angela," she was saying. "You were always an A student. But now you have become a C student. Why the downturn in grade average from last year? Are you having any specific difficulties?"

"No, ma'am," Angela answered, "I'm not having any more difficulties than usual. I can't explain it, Mrs. Bergmeier."

"Then maybe it is something at home that is bothering you. Is everything all right at home?"

"Everything is fine at home. What is disturbing me has nothing to do with what goes on at home. My parents and I get along fine."

"Well, then, perhaps it is something else. Care to talk about it? Maybe I can be of some help to you."

Angela tucked her head down and began chewing her fingernails. "No, I don't think you can. Nobody can...nobody."

"That's not so," Mrs. Bergmeier stated. "If you just come out with it then somebody might be able to tell you what you can do to help yourself."

"Nobody can help me at all. No one except God maybe."

"Oh, so that's it—a spiritual problem. Do you have anyone who can help you with it? A priest or pastor?"

Cringing, Angela wrapped her arms around herself in an effort to keep her emotions in. Mrs. Bergmeier was hitting too close. "I can't talk about it to anyone."

Mrs. Bergmeier was so determined to help the girl that she took another route. "Maybe if you could give me the phone number of your church, I can call your pastor, and you can confide in him. You do have a church, don't you?"

"Yes, but, please, Mrs. Bergmeier, don't call him. I don't want you to call him because—," she broke off before she could say that he was the cause of her problem.

"Angela, what is it? Won't you please tell me?"

Oh, well, I might as well, Angela thought to herself. It will make me feel better if I confide in her.

Looking up into her counselor's eyes, Angela said softly: "The senior minister of my church has been fooling around with me."

Mrs. Bergmeier was stunned for a moment. She took a breath and asked: "What do you mean by 'fooling around'?"

"I—I m-mean that I am his mistress."

❄

Florence was busy in her office. She and her husband worked for the same insurance company. She was a receptionist; Mark held an executive position and was frequently very busy and occupied. Florence had just transferred a call to one of the claims offices when the telephone rang again. It was Angela's guidance counselor, Mrs. Bergmeier. She said that she had some vital information about Angela, and could Mr. and Mrs. Sutton please come home so they could converse in private. This was not something she wished to discuss over the phone.

"I will try to get my husband over the switchboard," Florence responded. "I doubt if he can come home. He is in a very important meeting. Are you sure you can't discuss this now?"

"No, Mrs. Sutton, this is very serious. It must be talked about only in private. Can you meet me in about twenty minutes?"

"Very well. I'll see if I can get ahold of my husband. I'll meet you at our house in about twenty minutes."

Florence hung up the phone and glanced at the clock. It was quarter 'til two. She would have to ask her supervisor to get one of the secretaries to cover for her. Mrs. Bergmeier had said that what was to be discussed was so very serious that it could not be mentioned over the telephone. A feeling of apprehension welled up inside of Florence. What could it be? Was Angela in some sort of trouble? As she drove toward her house, she speculated as to what it could be. Drugs? No, Angela showed no signs of drug abuse. Then what?

Florence drove into the garage, stopped the car, turned the engine off and went into the house. She noticed that her daughter and the counselor had not yet arrived. She had been unable to get Mark. Oh, well, he will have to wait. She suddenly heard a car door slam and, looking out a window, noticed that Angela and Mrs. Bergmeier were coming up the front walk. The doorbell rang.

"Good afternoon, Mrs. Bergmeier," Florence said as she let them in. "I'm sorry, but I was unable to catch my husband. Can you still talk with me? Come on into the living room and sit down."

Mrs. Bergmeier and Angela followed Florence into the living room, but they remained standing, Mrs. Bergmeier with her hands on Angela's shoulders. Florence was about to offer them some lemonade but noticed that the mood was far too serious for any pleasantries.

"This is serious, isn't it?" Florence commented. "What is this all about? Why did you call me home?"

III

Mrs. Bergmeier looked down at Angela and then at the girl's mother. "Angela has something she wants to tell you. Go ahead, Angela dear."

Angela, however, was tongue tied, so her counselor spoke for her: "Mrs. Sutton, your daughter has informed me that the senior minister of your church has been sexually involved with her." She again looked at Angela with pity in her eyes.

Florence Sutton, on the other hand, stared in disbelief. What is this woman telling me? she asked herself. She then looked imploringly at her daughter, asking, "Could you please tell me what she is trying to say?"

Angela replied, "Dr. Barrett has taken me to be his mistress."

Florence gazed at her child incredulously. "What did you say?"

"I said that Dr. Barrett has made me his mistress."

Florence was as confused as ever. "I don't understand. What do you mean? What do you mean by 'mistress'?"

"I mean that Dr. Barrett makes me have sex with him."

"What do you mean 'makes you have sex with him'?"

"I mean just that, Mom. He makes me have sex with him."

Mrs. Bergmeier, watching the conversation between mother and daughter, added, "I believe, Mrs. Sutton, that your daughter is saying that the minister has been having sexual intercourse with your daughter. He has been using seduction, making demands, and manipulating her. This is a clear case of sexual abuse."

It suddenly dawned on Florence what was being said. It was too unbelievable! It was ridiculous, completely absurd! Sexual abuse? By a clergyman? That could never happen! Not a man like Dr. Ronald Barrett! This kind of thing happened only in a cult by a paranoid, deranged leader. This reminded her of the Reverend Jim Jones and his People's Temple. Or maybe someone like Jim Bakker or Jimmy Swaggart, whom she regarded as money-hungry hypocrites. But never a man like Dr. Barrett! It was too fantastic!

"That's absurd! A man like Dr. Barrett wouldn't even think of doing such a thing!" she stated.

"But it's true, Mom," Angela said humbly. "It has been going on since last summer."

Mrs. Bergmeier helped Angela explain further. "That's not all, Mrs. Sutton, there is more. Tell her, Angela."

Angela looked into her mother's eyes, which were full of disbelief and shock. "Mom, Dr. Barrett makes me pose for him."

"What do you mean 'pose'?"

"I mean he takes pictures of me wearing a bikini or maybe lingerie. And sometimes he takes photos of me in the nude. He uses an instant camera so he won't have to take the film out in public to be printed. That way no one will find out about the pictures."

This was all too much for Florence. What her daughter was saying sounded like something that came out of a "true confessions" magazine, one of those tabloids at the supermarket stand. Surely this could not be true!

Florence turned around, clasping and unclasping her hands. "I can't believe this is happening! I can't believe she is saying this! She is talking completely crazy! I can't believe she would say such things about a man of God!"

"But, Mrs. Sutton, your daughter is telling the truth, I believe," Mrs. Bergmeier said.

"But I can't believe it! It just cannot happen! A man like Dr. Barrett would not do such a thing! He is not that kind of person! He is the pastor of a dignified, respectable church!"

"Don't you believe me, Mom?" Angela looked at her mother pleadingly.

"No, I don't," Florence said simply.

"Then do you think your daughter is lying?" Mrs. Bergmeier asked.

"There is only one way to find out. Come, Angela, we will go have this out with our minister right now. I will show you how absurd your story is when we tell him what you said!" Florence marched Angela to the doorway while Mrs. Bergmeier followed.

"If I could be of any help...," the school counselor said.

"You have already helped enough by bringing this up. No, this is a matter for us to deal with. I think you should go on back to school. Let's go, Angela."

Mrs. Bergmeier left, and Florence and Angela walked toward the parsonage on Elmwood.

Angela walked along with her mother, thinking that this was the answer to her prayer the night before. Strange, but it did not seem to be working out the way she imagined it would. Her mother assumed that she was lying, that she was telling a story for some unknown reason. It did not make sense.

Florence rang the doorbell of the parsonage and waited for someone to answer. Joan Barrett came and greeted her guests.

"Well, good afternoon, Florence, Angela. Why you're home early today."

Good afternoon, Mrs. Barrett," Florence responded. "Is your husband at home? We must speak to him right away."

"No, I'm sorry, but he is at a conference on the other side of town right now, and he won't be back until about six or so. But his associate, Reverend Schiller, is over in his office. Maybe he can help you with whatever it is you need help on."

"No, we must see your husband," Florence stated firmly. "We will come back this evening."

"Maybe I can help you. Would you like to come in?" Joan held the door open wide for Florence and her daughter.

Angela and Florence entered and sat on the sofa where Joan motioned for them to sit. Their pastor's wife had dark brown hair, green eyes, and was of medium height. But she looked as though something had been bothering her, despite her efforts to conceal it. Joan offered her guests some lemonade and cookies, but they did not appear to be interested in refreshments. There was a look of tension about them.

"What is wrong?" Joan asked them. "You seem pretty serious about something."

Florence glanced at her child and then began: "I don't know really where to begin, Mrs. Barrett. You see, Angela, here, was brought home from school by her guidance counselor who said that Angela had something to tell me. Well, she, Angela, told me that ... um ... you see, she says that your husband has been ... I must try to put this delicately ... involved in some hanky-panky with her. You see what I'm trying to tell you?"

Joan Barrett wore the same expression on her face that Florence had when she first heard the news. It was a look of disbelief and amazement. "What do you mean by 'hanky-panky'?"

Angela then spoke up. "She means that your husband has been fooling around with me. You see, he makes me have sex with him."

Joan looked even more surprised and shocked than ever. "What do you mean he 'makes you have sex with him'? Do you mean that he has raped you?"

"No, not really, " Angela replied. "He has never forced me physically. But he says I must do it because it is God's will. I know that doesn't make sense, but it is what he said several times. Other times he said he would get me tickets to concerts and fairs. But usually, he just insists on it."

"That is not all, Mrs. Barrett," Florence said, 'Angela says that your husband has been taking pictures of her."

"Taking pictures?" queried Joan. "What kind of pictures?"

"Oh, pictures of me wearing lingerie—teddies, chemises— and a bikini," Angela explained. "And a lot of times he takes pictures of me in the buff. He uses an instant camera so he won't have to take the film to a photo processing center and anybody see the pictures."

Joan stared at her with an I-don't-believe-this look in her eyes. She recalled times when her husband, Ron she called him, insisted that she wear something sexy like lingerie along with glittering jewelry while they made love. She had always objected, saying that she felt cheap and that it took away the sanctity of the marriage relationship. And when he began making demands that she pose for him, well that was too much. Their marriage had deteriorated from then on. They were now sleeping at opposite ends of the bed. There had been no intimacy between them for over a year now.

"Young lady," she addressed Angela now, "do you realize what you are saying? You are insinuating that my husband has been committing adultery with you! Are you aware of that?"

Angela looked very shamefaced. "Yes, ma'am, I am."

"May I speak with you alone, Mrs. Sutton?" Joan asked Florence. "Come into the den."

Florence went with Joan into the den where Dr. Barrett usually spent his free time. Joan closed the door behind her so that they could talk without Angela hearing them.

"What your daughter has just told me is unbelievable."

"Yes, I agree with you, one hundred percent. Now why do you suppose she would say such things? Obviously they are not true. It is too fantastic!"

"I should say so. You see, Mrs. Sutton, my marriage has been going through rough times for the last year or so. Oh, Ron and I get along except for, well, our sex life. I would rather not go into that, of course. But if Ron were to have an affair with another woman, well, it would naturally be someone of age. At least closer to his own age. Your daughter is how old?"

"Fourteen in February."

"That is too young, even if she does look more mature. She looks more mature than Cheryl, and she is fifteen. They're only children by law."

"I have been thinking, Mrs. Barrett, that Angela must have become mentally unstable. She is imagining things and thinking that they are real! She has probably been influenced by these things we've been hearing about in the media about those TV evangelists—you know, Bakker and Swaggart."

"In other words Angela has lost touch with reality? Perhaps, then, you should take her to a therapist. She needs professional help."

"Thank you, I'll do that. Now I have to relate this to Mark when he comes home!"

Florence and Joan left the den and went back to the living room where Angela sat sipping a glass of lemonade.

"Come, Angela, we must go home now," Florence said. "Thank you for your time, Mrs. Barrett. We will see you next Sunday."

"What did you talk about, Mom?" Angela asked her mother as they left the parsonage.

"Never you mind, now," Florence replied. "We might as well get home now. You have schoolwork to do."

"Did she believe me?"

"No, she didn't. You ought to be ashamed of yourself for making up such stories!"

"But I'm not making it up, Mom!"

They had arrived home by now, and Angela was still insisting that she was being truthful and honest.

"Why would I lie to you? And why don't you want to believe me?"

Florence was taken aback by Angela's statement, for it suddenly occurred to her that her daughter just might be telling the truth. But because Dr. Barrett was such a good man on the outside, she could not believe it of him even if she tried.

"Dr. Barrett is a fine, decent, sane man, Angela. He is our pastor, a man of God! He is not some deranged leader of a crazy cult! And he is your best friend's father! Think how Cheryl will feel if she finds out that you have been telling lies about her own father!"

"But I'm not lying, Mom!" Angela cried, tears coming into her eyes. "And men of God can do such things. Look at Jim Bakker and Jimmy Swaggart."

"Dr. Barrett is not Jim Bakker! He is not Jimmy Swaggart! He is the senior pastor of a fine, respectable church! Now I don't want to hear any more from you about this! You go up to your room and stay there until I tell you to come down! And you put those wicked, blasphemous thoughts out of your mind! Dr. Barrett would not make you do what you said he has been doing. You're making all that up! You're lying!"

Angela rushed up the stairs to her bedroom, tears streaming down her cheeks. How could her own mother call her a liar? Why was she not believed? Her mother had always considered her honest and forthright.

Florence went up to her room and changed her suit for a housedress. How could Angela do such a thing, she wondered. Mark and I have brought her up right. She must be mentally and psychologically unstable. Why else would she make up a story like that and relate it as if it were real?

As Florence was going over recipes looking for something to fix for supper, the doorbell rang. On the porch stood two men who announced that they were police officers as they revealed their badges.

"We have had a report from a Mrs. Bergmeier that your daughter, age fourteen, is a possible victim of child abuse," said one officer named Lt. Callahan. "Your daughter's name is Angela. We would like to speak with her."

So Mrs. Bergmeier has called the police, Florence thought to herself. She did say to me that she believes Angela's story.

"I think you'd be wasting your time, officers," she stated. "My daughter doesn't know what she is talking about. She obviously has emotional problems. I believe she is making this up."

"Well, you may never know. The man she is accusing is a Dr. Ronald Barrett. He is a college professor or an M.D.?"

"He is a minister!"

"Oh, that kind of doctor. Well, clergymen can get in trouble just as much as the next person. Aren't we all human?"

"But I just can't believe he would do this sort of thing."

Angela had been listening to the conversation from the stairs. "Please, Mom, may I talk with them?"

Florence responded, "What are you doing out of your room? Didn't I tell you to stay put until I told you you can leave?"

But Angela was persistent. "Please, I would like to speak with them about this!"

"All right, you can come down."

Angela went into the living room, sat down on the sofa, and related to the police officers what she had told Mrs. Bergmeier, her mother, and Joan Barrett. Lt. Callahan nodded grimly while he took notes and asked questions. When Angela was finished, he said that they would go question Dr. Barrett.

"This is a clear-cut case of sexual abuse of a minor. Unless he gets treatment, he could spend several weeks in jail if convicted."

"Now that you're finished, Angela, you go right back up to your room," Florence told her daughter.

Angela complied, and Florence turned to the officers, who were starting to depart. "Do you really think that she is being truthful?"

"We can't say. We will have to question the accused. If he denies it, then it will be her word against his. But as for the possibility that she is making it up, I don't know. It would be an extremely exceptional child who would make up such a thing. It could just be that some other adult has put her up to a lie. Some adult member of your congregation who wants to get rid of Barrett."

Florence replied, "I can tell you that I don't know of anyone who might possibly be doing that. Everyone in our church loves Dr. Barrett and thinks the world of him."

"OK, thank you for your time, ma'am. Good day."

❄

After Angela and Florence had left the parsonage, Joan was in a state of perplexity. Could what Angela had just told her possibly be true? No, of course not! It was absurd! She was only fourteen years old! And she had said that this had been going on for nine months, which would mean that it began when she was only thirteen! Ron would never go for a girl so young, would he? Of course, Angela was quite mature physically for her age. But that did not stop the fact that she was their daughter's friend and still a child legally.

Shortly after three, Joan heard the doorbell ring. It was the two police officers who had just come from the Suttons', they said. They had had a report of child abuse brought against her husband, Dr. Ronald Barrett. Was he at home?

"He won't be home until after six," Joan responded. "Now, I think this is absurd. My husband is in the Lord's service. To think that he would abuse a child is ridiculous! He is a fine man. He cares for his family and his church! He is not a child abuser!"

"All the same, ma'am, we have to check it out. Do you and your husband have any children?"

"Yes, a son and a daughter. But what does that have to do with it?"

"You will have to get them out of the house, at least until your husband leaves the house. It is just possible that an abuser who abuses a child outside the family may be involved with his own children."

Oh, my God, Joan thought, this is too much. Help me, Lord, give me strength!

Meanwhile, down the street, the Barrett's two children, fifteen-year-old Cheryl and twelve-year-old Theodore, were on their way home from school. They noticed the police car in front of their home. They were both alarmed and curious.

"What's a cop car doing in front of our house?" asked Ted. "Do you think Mom and Dad are in some kind of trouble with the law?"

"I don't really know what kind of trouble they would be in since Dad is a man of the cloth," Cheryl replied. "The only possible thing that Dad might do against the law is get involved with the Sanctuary Movement."

"The what?"

"The Sanctuary Movement. This is where churches give protection to political dissidents from Central American countries like Guatemala or El Salvador. The church hides them from the immigration authorities."

"They hide them in the sanctuary of a church?"

"No, silly. They give them sanctuary by hiding them somewhere so that they can't be deported back to their own country where they would face possible execution."

The kids waited until the police car drove away before they entered the house. When they went in, their mother was waiting for them at the top of the stairs.

"You two home? Come upstairs, I have to get you packed."

Ted and Cheryl ascended the stairs. Joan explained to them that they were going to spend the night with their cousins. She had just called and arranged it for them.

"This is kind of sudden, Mom," Cheryl said. "Are you and Dad going to join us later?"

"No, it is just for the two of you."

Joan helped her children get their overnight bags packed, telling them that their aunt would be by in just a few minutes.

"Mom," asked Ted, "why were those two cops here? Is Dad in some kind of trouble?"

"Why do you ask?" Joan queried nervously.

"Well," Cheryl said, "we thought Dad might be involved with the Sanctuary Movement. We guessed this has something to do with Dad."

"Please, don't ask questions, now. I'll explain it all later when you come home tomorrow after school."

Aunt Sharon drove up in her car to pick up Cheryl and Ted. Joan kissed them both goodbye and they departed, leaving her in the quiet, empty house.

Joan glanced anxiously at the clock. It was 4:00; in about two hours her husband would be home. How would he react when she told him what Angela Sutton had revealed? Why would Angela say such things? There was no way they could be true. Oh, if only time would move more quickly so that she could talk to Ron!

IV

Florence had finished cooking dinner by 5:00 when Mark came home. She greeted him at the door, and he kissed her hello.

"I had word at the office that you wanted to speak with me while I was in conference," Mark said to her.

"Yes, it was urgent. You see, Angela's guidance counselor called me saying that she had to talk to us. I tried to get ahold of you but was unable to. Well, she said she had to speak with us right away." Florence followed her husband into his den. "I took the rest of the day off from work and came home. Angela and her counselor were waiting. What they had to say just absolutely shocked me. It explained what has been bothering Angela all these months."

"What was it?"

"Angela said that Dr. Barrett was quote 'making her have sex with him,' unquote."

"She said what?!" Mark exclaimed.

"That he makes her have sex with him. Isn't that ridiculous?! I can't figure out why she would make up something like that. I took her down to the parsonage. Dr. Barrett wasn't there, but his wife was. We talked. Angela related the same story to Joan Barrett. She couldn't believe it, either. When we came home I sent her up to her room and told her to stay there until I said she could leave."

"I'm surprised at Angela," Mark remarked. "She was always so honest and truthful. She has never done anything like this before."

"That's not all," Florence told her husband. "Two police officers came. Mrs. Bergmeier, Angela's counselor, called them, and they wanted to ask Angela some questions. I allowed her to come down and talk with them, and she told the same outrageous story she told Joan Barrett and me. She's in trouble if she gave false information to the police!"

"I should say she is."

"Mark, do you suppose there could be some truth to what she is saying? I know that sounds preposterous, but I can't help it right now. One of the officers who was here said it would be an exceptional child who would make up something like this."

"Maybe we have an exceptional child. We've always thought she was something unique."

"Well, it's time to eat. You might as well go tell Angela to get washed and come down for dinner."

Mark went upstairs and tapped on Angela's door, telling her to get ready for dinner. He asked his daughter how she was, and Angela could only mumble her reply.

All the way through the meal, Angela hardly said a word while Mark and Florence tried to keep up a lively conversation. Their daughter ate slowly, picking at her food.

"You're not eating too well, honey," Florence commented.

"I'm not very hungry, Mom," Angela replied.

"Your mother said you had a talk with your counselor today," Mark stated.

"I'd rather not talk about it, Dad, please."

Florence dismissed the issue, saying that they would discuss it another time.

❄

Joan Barrett hurried about fixing dinner after her children left the house for her brother's. She kept glancing nervously at the clock, waiting for her husband to arrive home. She began rehearsing to herself what she was going to say. She was very upset by what Angela Sutton had related to her about Ron. Surely the girl was making it all up! There could not be any truth to it, could there? Suppose there was? Well, the only way she could find out was by asking Ron himself. Of course, there would always be the possibility that he might lie if he were to deny the whole thing. But he would not do that, would he? Oh, if only he would get home!

At five past six, Ron drove into the garage and Joan breathed a sigh of relief. Now she could get to the bottom of this.

Fifteen minutes later they both sat at the table eating the leftovers Joan had warmed up. It was all she could fix, she explained to her husband.

"Where are Ted and Cheryl?" Ron asked her.

"They are over at their Uncle Bob and Aunt Sharon's. I sent them over there. Ron, there is something I must tell you. It is very serious. Angela and Florence Sutton came over here at about 2:30 this afternoon while you were away. Angela had something to tell you, but you, of course, weren't here."

Joan took a big breath and paused. This was going to be an extremely difficult thing to say, but she gave it all the courage she could muster.

"Angela Sutton says you've been having sex with her. Is that true?"

A look of shock came over Ron's features. He set his fork down and looked down at his plate saying nothing. He was quiet, he could not speak.

"Well, Ronald, what do you say?" his wife prodded him. "Why do you think Angela would say such a thing if it wasn't true?"

Still, Ron could not speak. The surprise was too much for him. He thought to himself, my sin has found me out, oh, God. What will I do now?

Joan by this time was becoming impatient. "I just can't understand that child! Making up a story like that! Why must she say things that aren't true?!"

At last Ron spoke: "Why else? It's true. That's why."

Joan could not believe her ears. "What did you say?"

"I said it is the truth—everything that Angela has said to you. I am as guilty as King David. And Angela is my Bathsheba."

What do I have here? Joan thought. He is talking crazy! I didn't expect this at all. I expected him to deny it, of course.

"Come now, Ron, you're out of your mind. You can't mean what you're saying!"

"I can and I do. It's all true. I've committed adultery with the Sutton girl. She is the Other Woman."

"But she is only fourteen! A mere child!"

"But she is also a woman. She's a woman-child."

"There's one more thing. The police were here this afternoon. Apparently, what you have been doing is against the law. They said it is sexual abuse of a minor. What do you have to say to that?"

Ron got up from the table and walked into the living room, his shoulders hanging dejectedly. "I'm sorry, Joan, dearest. I don't know what came over me. I hope you will understand. You did when I confessed to you about my encounter with Lt. Linda Barnes in Vietnam before we were married."

"I did understand then. An Army nurse in wartime is one thing. At least she was of legal age! But an adolescent like Angela!"

Ron closed his eyes as if in deep pain. "Please, Joan, not now. I have to figure out what to do. I should at least confess to the Suttons. I should tell them that their daughter is not making it up. And then I will go turn myself in to the police."

Joan broke down and wept. She could not believe this was happening. It had to be a nightmare, and maybe soon she would wake up. But it was no dream. It was real—the waking world. Ron patted her on the shoulder, telling her everything was going to be all right. He walked upstairs to their bedroom where he kept the evidence— the pictures he had taken of Angela with his instant camera. He reasoned that he should call the Suttons by telephone first and prepare them for what he had to say. Perhaps he would confess over the phone and then go over there and present them with the evidence before he went to the police station.

After dinner, Angela helped her mother clear the table and wash and dry the dishes. When they had completed this, the telephone rang. Mark went to answer it. Florence and Angela heard him speaking. "You're what? All right. We will be expecting you."

His wife and daughter came into the living room as Mark hung up. "That was Dr. Barrett. He's coming over. His wife told him about what Angela said. Florence, he confessed. He said that he's guilty of everything our daughter said he was guilty of." A stunned look had come over Mark's face. He looked as if he were sleepwalking.

Angela burst out: "I told you it was true! But neither of you believed me! You know I wouldn't lie about such a thing, but you kept insisting that I was making it up! You would not believe me!" She burst into tears, and sitting down on the sofa, she buried her face in her hands and sobbed as if her heart would break.

"You weren't lying, were you?" mused Florence. "It is true, isn't it? Oh, darling, we're sorry! It was just too unbelievable! Please forgive us!" Florence went over to her child, sat down beside her and embraced her, trying to comfort her.

Mark had come out of his trance, and anger replaced disbelief in his expression.

"Why did you let it happen, Angela?! Why did you let him do it? Couldn't you say no? Why did you say yes and let it go on?"

"I d-don't know, Dad," Angela sobbed. "I really don't know!"

"That is not a satisfactory answer, daughter," Mark said angrily. "Did you lead him on? What did you do? Answer me, you bimbo!"

Angela only cried harder at her father's harsh, angry words. Florence told him to stop, he was only making matters worse by tormenting Angela with such judgmental questions. She felt bad enough without all his condemnation!

The doorbell rang, and they knew it was Dr. Barrett. Angela said simply that she did not want to see him and ran upstairs to her bedroom. Mark let Dr. Barrett in, greeting him coldly. The minister told him why he had come—he wanted to apologize for what he did.

"It's all true, just like Angela said. Here are the photographs, some of them anyway. Apparently, you never knew that these were being taken. They were all done in private, of course."

Mark and Florence looked over the pictures. They were all in glossy color and were clear and very distinct. In many of them, Angela was wearing the rose-colored bikini she had bought the spring before. In others she was wearing lacy, sexy lingerie—Frederick's of Hollywood styles. In some of these, she also wore glittering jewelry and long white gloves. In other photos, she was entirely nude, lying on a bed or sofa.

Florence was indignant as she looked over the photos. "How could you do all this, Dr. Barrett? We trusted you. Naturally, we assumed you were a good man. How could you let us down?" She sat down on the sofa and wept just as her daughter had done.

Mark was as upset as his wife. "Yes, how could you do this?" he asked Dr. Barrett. "What do you have to say for yourself?"

"What else can I say? I'm sorry. I don't know what came over me. I tried to stop, but something just compelled me to go on. Pleasure, apparently. I knew it was wrong, but I acted impulsively. I don't know. I never thought I could do it. It just sort of came over me. I'm not asking for either of you to understand. I don't understand it myself. I'm going now to turn myself in to the police. I'll need those pictures."

Mark returned the photographs to Dr. Barrett, who then departed. He looked as if he had aged ten years since yesterday. He drove down to the police station where he confessed to his crime. Lt. Callahan booked him on a charge of child abuse, saying that Dr. Barrett was not to see any members of the Sutton family for the next thirty days until the county prosecutor could decide his case.

"But you can't do that!" Dr. Barrett objected. "I'm their pastor. They are part of my congregation."

"You are not to make any contact with any of them, especially the girl, for the next thirty days. Is that clear?"

Dr. Barrett relented. "Yes, sir."

❄

The rest of the week passed very quickly. Angela went to school and did her chores around home as if nothing had happened. Dr. Barrett moved out of his home and into a motel because of the difficulties he was having with Joan.

Angela wondered if everything that had happened for the past nine months with Dr. Barrett was finally over and done with. She still cringed whenever the telephone rang, and she was still afraid to be home alone. She remembered when Dr. Barrett would call her and ask if she was home alone or if she could "go out with friends." This is something he would say in order to get her to go out with him. She would have to tell her parents that she was "out with friends." Now, that all seemed to be over with—but she had a hard time convincing herself of that. It had gone on for so many months that she had become used to it by now.

Sunday arrived and Angela went to church with her parents filled with a sense of apprehension. What would Dr. Barrett say? she wondered. It was going to be hard to face him after what had transpired on Monday.

Angela, Mark and Florence sat with Mrs. Keller again when they gathered in the sanctuary for the 11:00 worship service. The opening hymn was "Holy, Holy, Holy," one of Angela's favorites. During the service, as the Old Testament lesson, Dr. Barrett read from II Samuel 12:1-7:

> The Lord sent Nathan to David. When he came to him, he said, "There were two men in a certain town, one rich and the other poor. The rich man had a very large number of sheep and cattle, but the poor man had nothing except one little ewe lamb he had bought. He raised it, and it grew up with him and his children. It shared his food, drank from his cup and even slept in his arms. It was like a daughter to him. Now a traveler came to the rich man, but the rich man refrained from taking one of his own sheep or cattle to prepare a meal for the traveler who had come to him. Instead, he took the ewe lamb that belonged to the poor man and prepared it for the one who had come to him." David burned with anger against the man

> and said to Nathan, "As surely as the LORD lives, the man who did this deserves to die! He must pay for that lamb four times over, because he did such a thing and had no pity." Then Nathan said to David, "You are the man!"

And for the New Testament lesson, I Corinthians 6:12-20:

> "Everything is permissible for me"—but not everything is beneficial. "Everything is permissible for me"—but I will not be mastered by anything. "Food for the stomach and the stomach for food"—but God will destroy them both. The body is not meant for sexual immorality, but for the Lord, and the Lord for the body. By his power God raised the Lord from the dead, and he will raise us also. Do you not know that your bodies are members of Christ himself? Shall I then take the members of Christ and unite them with a prostitute? Never! Do you not know that he who unites himself with a prostitute is one with her in body? For it is said, "The two will become one flesh." But he who unites himself with the Lord is one with him in spirit. Flee from sexual immorality. All other sins a man commits are outside his body, but he who sins sexually sins against his own body." Do you not know that your body is a temple of the Holy Spirit, who is in you, whom you have received from God? You are not your own; you were bought at a price. Therefore honor God with your body.

In his sermon, Dr. Barrett again related the story of David and Bathsheba, emphasizing David's repentance and subsequent chastening with the death of his son. He revealed that he, like David, was as guilty— with a member of the congregation.

"I will not reveal her name to you," he said. "It would cause her too much embarrassment, and she has suffered enough already. I want to now read to you from Psalm 51. It is David's psalm of repentance after his sin with Bathsheba."

Dr. Barrett read aloud from the Scriptures:

> Have mercy on me, O God, according to your unfailing love; according to your great compassion blot out my transgressions. Wash away all my iniquity and cleanse me from my sin. For I know my transgressions, and my sin is always before me. Against you, you only, have I sinned and done what is evil in your sight, so that you are proved right when you speak and justified when you judge. Surely I was sinful at birth, sinful from the time my mother conceived me. Surely you desire truth in the inner parts; you teach me wisdom in the inmost place. Cleanse me with hyssop, and I will be clean, wash me, and I will

> be whiter than snow. Let me hear joy and gladness; let the bones you have crushed rejoice. Hide your face from my sins and blot out all my iniquity. Create in me a pure heart, O God, and renew a steadfast spirit within me. Do not cast me from your presence or take your Holy Spirit from me. Restore to me the joy of your salvation and grant me a willing spirit, to sustain me. Then I will teach transgressors your ways, and sinners will turn back to you. Save me from bloodguilt, O God, the God who saves me, and my tongue will sing of your righteousness. O Lord, open my lips, and my mouth will declare your praise. You do not delight in sacrifice, or I would bring it; you do not take pleasure in burnt offerings. The sacrifices of God are a broken spirit; a broken and contrite heart, O God, you will not despise.

The congregation was shocked at Dr. Barrett's confession. They for the most part had thought him incapable of such an act. Mrs. Keller sat in her pew with her mouth a round O. The Suttons could hardly look at Angela, who was weeping as if her heart would break. She got up from her seat and walked out of the sanctuary into the hall leading to the fellowship hall. Florence started to go after her, but Mark held her back, saying that they could talk with her later.

Dr. Barrett wrapped up his sermon by saying that his flock was no doubt disappointed in him and even surprised. "It shows how little we actually know about each other. You no doubt thought me incapable of such behavior. I'm sorry I let all of you down. I also want to tell you that I am resigning my position here. Reverend Schiller will take over for me until a new senior pastor can be appointed. I know he will do well taking my place." Dr. Barrett closed his Bible and started to leave his pulpit. "I just want to say I'm sorry, and I hope you will forgive me." And, as he could no longer hold back the tears, he left the sanctuary.

Reverend Schiller led the congregation in prayer. They prayed that they would forgive their pastor for the way he had wronged them. And they prayed for the unnamed female in the church with whom he had sinned. Mark and Florence and the Barretts knew who it was so they prayed for Angela. They tried not to judge her since they knew how miserable she felt. The poor child! How could her own parents and her best friend sit in judgment on her?

When Dr. Barrett moved out of the parsonage, the previous Tuesday, his son and daughter asked why he had done so. Joan explained about the visit from the police on Monday. She revealed to her children the crime their father had been charged with. She explained what he had done and what Angela had told them. They were suddenly quiet. Ted went to his room, but Cheryl looked as if she would weep.

"How could she say such things?! Why did she let him do it? Why did he do it? Oh, I can't believe this!" She burst into tears and ran up to her room. Joan followed her daughter and tried to comfort her.

"I hate her!" cried Cheryl. "I hate them both! How could my best friend and my own father do this?!"

"You must not say such things. You'll only regret them later."

Now as Cheryl sat in church, having heard her father's confession and having watched her friend run out, she felt remorseful at the words she had uttered on Tuesday. She wanted to forgive them both, but right now she felt a little hesitant about facing either one of them. Perhaps it was because of the guilt she felt for having felt that she hated them. She prayed with the rest of the people that she would find it in her heart to pardon her father and her friend.

V

That afternoon Joan tried to get her mind off her troubles by cleaning out the parsonage attic. She started with the old furniture they had stored up there when they bought new. She figured she could donate them to charity. Next she began going over old boxes that had been stored a long while. As she was moving a box from out of a corner, she came across an old cedar chest. She gazed at it, not remembering when she had seen it last. Then she remembered. It was the chest her parents had given Ron and her as a wedding present seventeen years before. But she could not recall when it had been placed up here in the attic. Never mind, she decided, better see what's inside.

She looked around for the key, and found it hanging on a peg on the wall above. She unlocked the chest, her heart pounding with curiosity as to what was in it. She gasped with horror. She could not believe her eyes. Magazines—dozens of them. Not ordinary magazines normally found in a Christian home, but "soft-core" pornographic magazines. There were issues of *Playboy* and *Penthouse,* dating back two years. It was just too unbelievable, so absurd. Could this have played any part in what Ron did to Angela Sutton? She recalled studies which showed that pornography—both "soft-core" and "hard-core"—had an effect on the man or youth who was addicted to it. He would often be compelled to act out the fantasy material he was looking at and reading. The pornographic materials would have an effect on his brain. Sensations of pleasure would induce a hormone secretion in the brain. This would cause addiction and enslavement to reading erotic books and looking at pornographic pictures and watching "adult" movies and videos. But Joan Barrett was nonetheless shocked and horrified that her own husband would be a pornography addict.

It was the answer for everything. The times he asked her to dress up in flimsy, sexy lingerie. And the times he would ask if she would pose for him while he photographed her wearing the lingerie or wearing nothing at all. Of course, she refused. Was this what drove him to Angela? She was willing to pose for him, and he pressured and bribed her to do it because his wife would not. Blinding rage filled her heart. She sat down on the floor in an effort to control herself. The next time she saw Ron she would confront him about what she had found in this cedar chest.

Joan went downstairs and, trying to console herself, sat down at the piano and played some popular songs from the days when she was young. One of the songs she played was "Yesterday." It was one of her favorites, and the words conveyed what she was feeling right now. Later she played "Can't Help Falling in Love." This was the song that was sung at her wedding seventeen years before. Playing that broke her heart, and as the tears came into her eyes, she got up from the piano bench and went to take one of the tranquilizers she had started taking a few days before. Then she went to her bedroom to have a good cry.

That evening after dinner, Joan was cleaning out the cupboards in the kitchen when she heard the doorbell ring. Upon opening the door, she was surprised to find her husband standing there.

"What are you doing here, Ron?" was all she could say.

"I want to talk with you. I know you heard me in church this morning, but I want to say to you that I am giving up the ministry in a few weeks. That is, I'm not going to pastor a church anymore."

"Oh, well, it's your decision. What will you do then?"

"I've applied for an administrative position at a college and seminary back in Pennsylvania. It belongs to our denomination."

"Well, I hope you get it."

Ron noticed something about Joan. She was quite on edge about something.

"Joan, is there anything bothering you? You seem very upset over something this evening."

"Yes," she replied, "there is. Ronald, I cleaned out the attic this afternoon. I found something of yours."

"Something of mine?"

"Yes, something of yours. I don't think they belong to Ted, since we know he wouldn't buy such magazines after we told him not to."

"Magazines?"

"You don't have to pretend, Ronald Barrett. I know now that you have been secretly buying that filth and keeping it hidden up there. Oh, how could you?! After you preached to your children and others about pornography! I never thought that you would do such a thing! Well, you know very well I became upset. After I managed to calm down, I took that trash, put it all in a trash bag and threw it in the garbage can where I hope no innocent child gets ahold of it."

"I thought you would never know. I'm sorry, Joan. I —"

"How many times are you going to say you're sorry? After all we've been through this past week! I've started taking tranquilizers, which explains why I'm not running up and down the neighborhood screaming my head off! This whole week has been a nightmare that may never end!"

"Look, Joan, please try to understand."

"Understand? Understand what?" Joan's voice rose to a high shrill. "That you, a man of God, have been secretly buying and keeping pornographic magazines, and that you seduced a member of your congregation! A fourteen-year-old child at that!"

"Please, Joan, I said ...," Ron reached out for Joan's hand, but she backed away, recoiling from him as if his presence repulsed her.

"Don't you touch me!" she cried, "You are a hypocrite! A Pharisee! You are a white-washed tomb filled with dead men's bones! Clean and pure on the outside but filled with filth on the inside! You're disgusting! I hate you! I hate you for what you did! I hate you for what you are! I hate you for it! I do! I do!" Joan collapsed on the porch step and sobbed aloud. She could not be consoled, she was so afflicted.

Ronald walked away, his heart like a weight of lead in his chest. If only he could reach her! But she was not to be reasoned with in her present state of mind. Please, God, he prayed, help her to forgive me. Forgive me, please, Lord.

❄

The next afternoon, Angela was in her room doing her homework when Mrs. Keller dropped by.

Florence greeted her friend at the front door. "Won't you come in, Audrey? Come with me into the living room and we'll talk. How have you been doing?"

But Mrs. Keller had something on her mind. She looked as if she wanted to talk serious business.

"Where is Angela?" she asked. "I wish to speak to the both of you."

Florence called Angela down and told her Mrs. Keller wanted to talk with them.

"I'll get straight to the point," Audrey Keller began. "I noticed, Angela, the way you rushed out of the sanctuary yesterday morning. You were in tears, it was obvious. Now I don't mean to pry, but is it you?"

"What do you mean, Mrs. Keller?" Angela queried.

"Oh, don't play innocent with me, young lady. You know very well what I mean. I just would like to know one thing—are you Dr. Barrett's Other Woman? Well, are you?"

Angela was taken aback by this. She knew Mrs. Keller was sharp in her way of figuring out things but never expected this. She lowered her eyes in shame and responded: "Yes, I am."

"Ah ha," exclaimed Mrs. Keller, "I might have known. The way you carry on!"

"What do you mean 'carry on'?"

"You know. That bikini you wore last summer. Always trying to look seductive!"

Florence interrupted, "Audrey, Angela wore that suit because she says that all the girls wear them, although I disagree."

To Florence's surprise, Mrs. Keller then turned on her. "You shouldn't have bought it for her! You have the responsibility of bringing her up right! But look at what happened. She entices an older man! She leads him on! And a man of God, too! Well, I have never in all my born days seen the like! A girl brought up by such fine parents turns out to be a slut!"

Angela could not bear to hear any more. She rushed upstairs before the tears could flow and entered her room, slamming the door.

Florence was indignant that a friend of the family would behave in such a manner. To hurl such accusations at her daughter!

"If you have nothing more to say, Audrey Keller, then you may leave! I'll gladly show you the door!"

"That's fine with me! I just came here to say my piece, and now that I've said it, I shall take my leave!" She left through the front door, which Florence slammed behind her.

❊

After her encounter with Mrs. Keller, Mark and Florence knew without a doubt that Angela needed some professional counseling. There was a counseling center in town that was a Christian counseling center. It was called Our Healer Counseling. Florence made an appointment for Angela to meet with a counselor by the name of Miss Marvin the next day, Tuesday.

When Angela entered the counseling center, she noticed a plaque on the wall that displayed a portion of Scripture from Isaiah 53:5: "By his stripes we are healed." Angela had heard many of the "name-it-claim-it" preachers on TV quote that verse as a "proof text" for the belief that physical healing was part of Christ's atonement. But her Sunday School teacher told her that it was spiritual, not physical, healing that the passage referred to. Angela grew nervous as the time for her session grew near. What would Miss Marvin think of her? The counselor might never have had a case like Angela's before. When at last Miss Marvin came for Angela, the girl drew a deep breath and walked toward the counseling room.

Miss Marvin had red hair and brown eyes. She was about thirty-five years old and lived alone with her pet cocker spaniel. Angela commented that her family had had a cocker, a light-brown one, for about fifteen years. The dog died when Angela was twelve.

"Your mother explained your situation to me. She told about what happened with the pastor of your church."

"Oh?" Angela said blushing. "I suppose you have never had anyone like me before."

"How do you mean?" asked Miss Marvin.

"I mean someone who would do what I did."

Miss Marvin sat down next to Angela, patted her on the hand, and said compassionately, "You haven't done anything."

"I haven't?" Angela asked.

"No, you haven't done anything wrong. The wrong has been done to you. You were a victim, not an offender."

"I see. But my case is still one of a kind. I have heard about women who had affairs with ministers, but I'm a kid."

"Angela," Miss Marvin said soothingly, "what happened to you is not as rare as you think. It is more common than most people assume. Girls of all ages, some a little older than you, some a bit younger, have gone through similar ordeals. They come from various economic, racial, and denominational backgrounds. They're Protestant, Catholic, and Pentecostal, any brand you can name. There are even instances in which boys are involved. So your situation is not unique."

"Angela was amazed, but at the same time comforted to learn this. "I thought that I was the only one."

"But you are not. Now, suppose you tell me about your relationship with Dr. Barrett."

Angela began with the time she first met the Barretts, four years earlier. She and Cheryl became fast friends. The parsonage was only a few blocks down from Angela's house, so she could go see Cheryl every day—meaning that she also saw Cheryl's father almost every day.

"I suppose it all started when I pressured my folks to buy me a string bikini. I told them that all the other girls wear them, except Cheryl. But, then, I wanted to conform. Cheryl, being a preacher's kid, felt she shouldn't wear one. Mom got me the bikini, all right. I wore it to the pool and to the lake every time starting last Memorial Day."

Angela went on to say that Cheryl had a set-up swimming pool in her yard and that she spent a lot of time there. One time Dr. Barrett was there in the back yard. He offered to take some pictures of her while Cheryl went into the house for some lemonade. Angela consented. He used an instant camera. But it did not end there. Over the next week or two, Dr. Barrett began calling Angela on the telephone, asking her if she would be home alone or if she would come over to his place. He would make more photographs. At first, Angela wore the bikini, but later she would wear some lingerie: teddies, chemises, lacy underwear, and she also wore jewelry and sometimes long white gloves. After a time, she would be told to remove the bikini or lingerie. She then would be photographed in the nude. Dr. Barrett said he would keep the pictures hidden, and he instructed her not to tell anyone about the photograph sessions.

"When was the first time he touched you?" Miss Marvin inquired of Angela.

"It was about two weeks after he first photographed me in the bikini," Angela replied. "You see, I was at Cheryl's, and we had had a terrible argument. I left her and started to go home. I started crying and went instead over to the church building where I hoped her dad would be. I thought maybe I could talk to him, and he could comfort me. I just wanted him to comfort me and hold me close the way my father used to do before I grew up."

"What do you mean 'the way your dad used to do'?"

"I don't know why, but Dad never hugs me or cuddles me at all. I would like him to. At least when I am sad or when I cry. Why, even when my dog died or when my Grandfather Allison died, Dad didn't hug me or anything when I cried over it. He just patted me on the shoulder and said it would be all right.

"Well, I went to Dr. Barrett's office hoping I would find him there. I did. I started to tell him about my fight with Cheryl, but I only cried harder. He took me into his arms and hugged me, patting me on the back. He stroked my hair and caressed my cheeks. He took out a handkerchief and wiped my face. And then he kissed me. It was not the kind of kiss I expected. You know, on the cheek. No, he kissed me fully on the mouth like a lover."

"How did that make you feel?"

"Strange. I had never been kissed by a grown man before. Oh, some boys at school, the ninth graders, tried to kiss me. But I always stopped them.

"Well, then Dr. Barrett took me up on his lap as he sat down in the chair behind his desk. Then he began fondling me. He caressed my breasts, and he stroked my thighs—I was wearing short shorts that day."

"How did that make you feel?"

"I wondered if that was something he should be doing. I didn't tell anyone, of course."

"When and where did he first have intercourse with you?" Miss Marvin queried.

"It was about two weeks after that. It was in my bedroom. My parents had gone out to a garden party that afternoon. They were going to be late coming home, and they promised to bring home some Kentucky Fried Chicken. Well, Dr. Barrett as usual brought his camera over and took pictures of me. After the picture taking, it happened."

"How did you feel about that?"

"It was a bit painful at first. It's supposed to be, but I sort of liked it after that. Does that make me a bimbo?"

"No, dear. Go on."

"When he was finished, he told me that it was supposed to happen. He said that it was God's will. He warned me not to tell anyone because no one would understand, especially Mrs. Barrett."

"How often did he have intercourse with you after that?"

"Oh, about twice a week, at least that often. After the first time, I was afraid of getting pregnant. But he gave me some contraceptive sponges that his wife used to use. I didn't know how to put one in, so he inserted it for me that first time. He said it would fix things fine, and that I didn't have to worry.

"He told me a lot of things to get me to do it with him. He would open the Bible to the Song of Solomon. He said it is a very sexy book. He said people in Bible times were very frank and open about sex, and that our generation was still very prudish and Victorian. He read passages from the

Song of Solomon, and they did sound what he called erotic. There is a part that talks about the Shulammite's breasts being like young deer or something like that. And there is a part which says she is like a palm tree and her breasts are like its clusters of grapes. Dr. Barrett said that was what my figure looked like. I was flattered because he was saying that I was sexy.

"He showed me another portion of Scripture. It was Hebrews 13:17. It said that rulers are to be obeyed. He interpreted this to mean that even pastors are to be obeyed. He meant that I should obey him and have sex with him whenever he wanted it.

"He showed me something out of *National Geographic.* It was about Charles Dickens. The article said that he was friends with a young actress named Ellen Ternan, who was young enough to be his daughter. But Dr. Barrett revealed to me what he had heard on that PBS program, *Masterpiece Theatre.* He heard the program's host, Alistair Cooke, say that this actress was really Dickens's mistress. That is what he said. Anyway, he said that everyone has sex outside of marriage, and that men and women need sexual fulfillment. I believed him, of course. I didn't know what else to think. I get confused whenever I remember all this."

Tears were streaming down Angela's cheeks. Miss Marvin handed her a tissue to dry her face.

STOP

Read Friday 05/19/96 p. 37-56

VI

"How do you feel about your pastor now?" the therapist asked Angela.

"I can't really say," Angela replied. "I still love him, but at the same time I feel angry with him and disappointed in him. There was one time, I believe it was last October on World Communion Sunday, when we were taking communion in our church, and when I was finished, I looked at Dr. Barrett and I burst out crying and ran from the sanctuary. You see, I remembered a verse, I Corinthians 11:27, which says that if anyone partakes of the cup and the bread in an unworthy manner, he sins against the body and blood of Christ. And I knew then that that was what Dr. Barrett and I were doing. I felt so wicked! I couldn't contain myself.

"There was this one time when I wanted to go to an Amy Grant concert, but my parents said that I would have to save my allowance. Well, I didn't have enough money for tickets when the time came for the concert. Dr. Barrett said he would buy tickets for me *if...* well, you know what I mean. He would bribe me like that.

"I remember once when I was babysitting for Travis Clark—he's the son of some members of our church. Well, somehow Dr. Barrett found out where I was, and he came over to the Clarks' where I was. He had his camera with him along with a pink chemise. He made me put the chemise on and pose for him. I knew perfectly well where all this was going to lead. Well, right in the middle of the picture-taking, little Travis comes downstairs asking for a drink of water. I was scared the kid would notice something, and he did. After I gave Travis his drink and started to carry him back to bed, he said 'It's the doctor from the church. What's he doing here?' I told Travis never mind and took him back to bed. I was never so frightened before in my life. I was afraid Travis would tell his parents that Dr. Barrett had been there, and that I was wearing 'something different from what I had had on.' Of course, I sort of hoped we would be found out so that it would come to an end. But then there would always be the consequences if we were discovered. I feared that the Barretts' marriage would be on the rocks. And then I would be to blame for their family breaking up. At least, that was the way I felt."

"You had quite an ordeal, didn't you?" Miss Marvin commented. "Tell me, can you forgive Dr. Barrett for what he did?"

"I want to. The Bible says that Christians should be loving and forgiving each other as God through Christ has forgiven us. But I think it will be so hard to forget. I often wonder how it will affect my future. I worry about how I might feel about sex if and when I marry. Will I feel guilty when my husband makes love to me?"

"That is why you need counseling, honey. Your parents were smart to get you in here."

On Thursday Miss Marvin spoke with Mark and Florence. She related how her first meeting with Angela had gone. She asked the Suttons if they had any questions to ask her concerning Angela's case.

"What we still don't understand," stated Florence, "is how a man like Dr. Barrett could do such a thing. We didn't think incidents such as these occurred in churches like ours."

Miss Marvin smiled understandingly. "You see, the paranoid cult leader with a Messiah complex is a misconception far too many people have concerning a sexually-abusive clergyman. It can happen in any traditional, orthodox, respectable church. You say you don't know how he could have done it. My guess is that he is weak-willed. Another guess is maybe he has a secret addiction to something like pornography. I admit I don't know everything about him so I can't answer for him."

She went on to comment that Angela had mentioned her father's lack of demonstrative affection for her. Mark squirmed when the therapist brought this up. Angela was so beautiful and so mature that Mark was afraid of unfatherly feelings for her. Many times he would refuse to look at her when she wore her bikini.

"I remember how I felt when I saw her come downstairs for that dance a week ago. And I kept thinking what it would be like... well, I wished that I could be her partner," Mark said haltingly. "Then I felt ashamed since she is my daughter."

Miss Marvin looked sympathetically at Mark. "Every one of us has, at some time or another, an incestuous thought. Normally it is just fleeting and often unbidden, and doesn't mean that we're going to act on it. Most people, of course, don't act on it. But you need not be so afraid of your daughter as to withhold your affection. She has had the idea that you don't love her anymore."

Mark looked stricken. "I had no idea she felt that way. I will try to make it up to her. I won't tell her how I felt, though. She might become afraid of me."

"No she won't," Miss Marvin interjected. "She will understand."

❄

By the next Sunday word had spread about Angela. It was Mrs. Keller who was responsible. She who had been such a good friend of the Suttons had turned on them. She continued to think that Angela was to blame for Dr. Barrett's actions, although she sat in judgment on him as well despite his plea for forgiveness. Several of the Suttons' loyal friends brought word of this to Reverend Schiller, who decided to use this issue on Sunday in his sermon.

That Sunday morning he used as his sermon topic John 8:1-11:

But Jesus went to the Mount of Olives. At dawn he appeared again in the temple courts, where all the people gathered around him, and he sat down to teach them. The teachers of the law and the Pharisees brought in a woman caught in the act of adultery. They made her stand before the group and said to Jesus, "Teacher, this woman was caught in the act of adultery. In the Law Moses commanded us to stone such women. Now what do you say?" They were using this question as a trap, in order to have a basis for accusing him. But Jesus bent down and started to write on the ground with his finger. When they kept on questioning him, he straightened up and said to them, "If any one of you is without sin, let him be the first to throw a stone at her." Again he stooped down and wrote on the ground. At this, those who heard began to go away one at a time, the older ones first, until only Jesus was left, with the woman still standing there. Jesus straightened up and asked her, "Woman, where are they? Has no one condemned you?" "No one, sir," she said. "Then neither do I condemn you," Jesus declared. "Go now and leave your life of sin."

Angela was startled by Reverend Schiller's reading of this passage of Scripture. She had a sudden feeling that it was somehow connected with her. She looked at Mrs. Keller who was now seated in a pew across the aisle, instead of with her and her parents. Oh, God, Angela prayed, help Mrs. Keller to see what your Word says to her. Open her eyes and help her to forgive and forget.

Reverend Schiller was now saying, "Some people often use this verse to either condone or at least take a neutral stand on morality and right and wrong. This is done not only in the secular world, but too often in the church. This verse is often quoted to promote moral relativism. But that is not the issue here. The Lord is not saying 'do not point out sin and call sin by its name.' He is saying that we must not condemn someone who is repentant, and that we must examine ourselves first.

"Right now in this church, we have a similar situation. Our former senior pastor and a young girl in this congregation were caught in the same kind of sin. Although it wasn't really the girl's fault. Let us not hold it against them. They are both repentant and sorry. Each of them is seeking or planning to seek help because of what happened.

"In closing I want to say that Christians must be forgiving toward each other for the wrongs they have committed. Forgive one another just as God in Christ has forgiven us. Amen."

Later, as the congregation rose to sing the closing hymn, Angela glanced at Mrs. Keller across the aisle. The elderly woman appeared to be wiping her eyes. Did she have something in her eye, or was she wiping away tears of repentance?

That afternoon the Suttons were sitting in the front yard after a rain shower had passed through. The lilac blossoms, with their colors of lavender and white, were still in bloom although they would soon be "rusting" after two weeks on the branch. Florence had just clipped a bouquet of tulips when she noticed Mrs. Keller coming down the street.

"Good afternoon, Audrey," Florence greeted her friend. "I'm glad you've decided to come see us."

"Yes," Mrs. Keller replied, "it's about the other day. You know, when I spoke so harshly to Angela. I just want to say that I'm sorry. May I speak to Angela personally?

"Here I am, Mrs. Keller," Angela spoke up and walked over to greet the friend of her parents. "I think I know what you're about to say, and it's all right."

"Oh, bless you, child," Mrs. Keller cried, her voice choking up. "I was so afraid you would hate me. I'm really sorry for the way I treated you last week. Will you forgive me? I was very cruel, really I was."

Angela embraced Mrs. Keller, saying that she had forgiven her. "You just didn't understand that I was victimized. I had the same thoughts about myself as you did. I thought that I was so bad and sinful. It wasn't really my fault."

"Well, even if it had been, I shouldn't have sat in judgment on you as you would have been repentant. But, instead, I was the wicked one." She returned Angela's embrace and wiped her eyes. Looking down at the girl, she smiled at her, saying what lovely blue eyes she had.

❄

The county prosecutor decided not to press charges against Dr. Barrett, partly out of respect for his profession but also because Dr. Barrett decided to get therapeutic help at the counseling center where Angela was getting treatment. The Suttons referred him to Miss Marvin, saying she was an excellent counselor.

When Dr. Barrett entered Miss Marvin's office, he was at first embarrassed to explain what his problem was. He knew that the therapist knew Angela, and he described himself as the man who had victimized her.

"Would you like to begin telling me how it all started?" Miss Marvin prompted Dr. Barrett.

"I don't know exactly how or when it all started," he began. "Maybe it was way back when I was fourteen, Angela's age."

"Oh, would you care to talk about it?"

Dr. Barrett started by explaining about his childhood. He was the oldest son. He had three sisters and two brothers. Like himself, his father was a

Methodist minister, and his mother was a housewife. Unlike so many mothers today, she was always at home when the children needed her. She was a kind, sympathetic and understanding woman. But his father was a little different. He was quite a perfectionist, and a bit conservative. While it was good that he had a conservative theology, Ronald thought, his attitude toward boys showing emotion was overly "macho." But what was most troublesome was the way he reacted to Ronald's possession of a "skin" magazine at the age of fourteen.

Ronald was home with some of his friends one Saturday. They were looking through a catalog with pictures of women in swimsuits. One of the boys remarked that he knew where they could really see something revealing in the manner of women's bodies. Ronald asked where and the other boy, nicknamed Red, went home and came back with a magazine in his hand.

"What kind of magazine is that?" Ron asked.

"Wait 'til you see," Red replied.

He held the magazine by one end, spread it out and held it up to the wall. It contained a centerfold spread of a young, voluptuous beauty wearing nothing at all.

"How do you like her?" Red asked.

Ron was tongue-tied. He felt embarrassed and at the same time excited. But he could not say how he felt, not even to his friends.

"I think you'd better take it back home, Red," he commented.

"Ah, come on, don't be a prude, Ron. Just because you're a preacher's kid."

Ron did not know what else to say. What if his father suddenly came into the room and found Red with the centerfold in his hands? Of course, William Barrett would know his son was not to blame for Red's actions. But still Ron did not want Red to get caught.

In the weeks that followed, Ron tried to keep that picture out of his mind. But, to his frustration, he found he could not. He went over to Red's house and asked if he had any more of those magazines. Red had some back issues that Ron could have for free. Ron took the magazines home and hid them under his bed. Whenever he felt like it, he would take them out and look over them. There were photographs of women nude and semi-nude. Ron knew such magazines existed, but he had never seen them before.

As Ron grew older, he found the magazines irresistible. He bought some of his own and would take them out of hiding whenever he wanted to look at them. Then the blow came. One afternoon, William Barrett burst in on his son while Ron was doing his homework in the den. In William's hand was one of the *Playboy* magazines that Ron had purchased and was hiding in his room.

"Where did you get this, young man?" William's question had the ring of a demand.

"I—I bought it, sir," Ron replied.

"You bought it! You spent your allowance money on this filth?"

"Yes, sir."

"Do you know what this is, son? This is pornography! This is for men with evil minds. Men who look at women with lust in their eyes! You know what Christ said in the Sermon on the Mount about looking on a woman to lust after her. It is in Matthew 5:28. That verse says that if a man looks upon a woman to lust after her, he has committed adultery with her in his heart!"

Ron looked shamefacedly down at his papers. He could not even look his father in the face. "I know, Dad."

"Well, now, son, you just take all that trash and throw it in the garbage can. And I don't ever want to see you possessing it again! Do you hear me?"

"Yes, sir."

Ron did as he was told. He took all the *Playboy* magazines, made a pile of them and threw them out in the garbage. He tried to make a vow to himself that he would never buy one again. When he went back into the house, his father had something else for him to do. He was to write Philippians 4:8 two hundred times on a piece of paper. Ron sat down and complied.

> Finally, brethren, whatsoever things are true, whatsoever things are honest, whatsoever things are just, whatsoever things are pure, whatsoever things are lovely, whatsoever things are of good report; if there be any virtue, and if there be any praise, think on these things.

Ron thought at one point as he was writing: What could be more lovely than those girls in those magazines.

But as the months and years passed, Ron found that he could not keep the "filth" out of his mind. In later years, he figured that the way his father handled the subject was what triggered his desire to seek more erotic magazines. William did not sit down with Ron patiently and explain why the "filth" was so bad, that it makes sex objects out of women. No, the manner in which William had dealt with the situation suggested that he was some Victorian prig. At least that was the way Ron saw it back then.

During the rest of his adolescent years, Ron continued to purchase "girlie" magazines. He hid them better than before in order to make sure his parents would not find them. The pictures were so exciting! He began to fantasize about making love to beautiful sexy women like Marilyn Monroe and Jayne Mansfield. He started having erotic, sexually-arousing dreams. He never told anyone about these fantasies or dreams because he feared that he would be told he was having "evil thoughts." In his early and middle teens, Ronald Theodore Barrett did not understand that thoughts and fantasies can often lead to the acting out of those daydreams and thoughts. There were times, however, when Ron felt so guilt-ridden that he would throw away the magazines, telling himself that he would never again buy or even look at them. But after a while, once Ron had thought he had been victorious over his "lust," he would just go back to the old habit.

After graduation from high school and college attendance, Ronald entered the seminary to study for the ministry. He wanted to follow in his father's footsteps. During this period, he had to be very careful about his secret habit of buying "girlie" magazines. For a seminary student to be discovered with porn magazines would be devastating. He could even be expelled if his weakness was ever uncovered. But he continued to buy and hide them. He was never found out.

There was one seminary professor in whom Ron had great trust. He confided to this professor about his habit and his fantasies. Ron did not say that he had any magazines in his possession for fear of reprisal. The professor merely advised to pray that God would "keep the filth out of your head." He presented no further advice. Ron tried it, but felt that he could learn to overcome his bad habit by himself. When he did pray to God to take away his habit, it worked, but only for a while. Ron guessed it was because he did not pray for the habit to stay away.

The same year that Ron was ordained, he was drafted. This was during the period of the Vietnam war, and Ron, unlike many other young men, felt proud to be serving his country. He went into the Army as a chaplain, and he was sent to Vietnam for two years. While serving on base, he frequently went over to the base hospital to meet with the wounded. It was during this time that he met an Army nurse, Lt. Linda Barnes. She had blonde hair and azure-blue eyes, and she stood tall and graceful. She and Ron were attracted to each other immediately, although they did not consider marriage. Over the next two years, they saw each other, and they went out on dates to the clubs. It was during his last month in Vietnam, Ron recalled, that his weakness suddenly caught up with him. In order to keep up his reputation as a base chaplain, he had to stay away from publications like *Playboy* and *Penthouse* which many other soldiers managed to get hold of. His abstinence, however, increased the frustration which soon boiled over.

VII

One evening at the base hospital, Ron had been speaking with and counseling the wounded. At the same time, Lt. Barnes was on duty at the hospital. They met and conversed for a while before going off duty. When off-duty time came, they made love in a supply room in an isolated section of the building. It just came over him, the desire and the will to do it, Ron reasoned. He knew it was wrong, and so did she, but they could not help themselves. It was an act of unbridled passion. When it was all over, Ron hated himself. He apologized to Lt. Barnes, saying that it should never have happened. He called her Linda for the first time, too. Ron felt worried that someone would find out about their fornication, which would be a terrible predicament for a base chaplain. Linda said not to worry, she would preserve their little secret. Looking back, Ronald Barrett thought this was a harbinger of what was to happen with Angela—the first hidden scarlet sin he covered up in order to protect his reputation as a man of God.

After his service in Vietnam, Ron returned to civilian life and to pastoring a church. He was appointed associate pastor to a large church in Kansas City where he met his future wife. Joan Caldwell was pretty, twenty-two years of age and a recent graduate of the College of Education at the University of Missouri at Columbia. She was a first-grade teacher at a local public school. Ron, or Reverend Barrett as he was now known, and Joan fell in love at first sight. They began dating almost immediately and vowed they would get married some day. Ron managed to control himself this time, largely out of respect for Joan. They were married one-and-a-half years later, and as Ron stayed an associate pastor for one more year, Joan was happy to be his wife. A year after their marriage, Ron was appointed the pastor of a small congregation in Pierce City, Missouri. It was here that, several months later, Cheryl was born. Three years later, Theodore was born. Joan had continued to work as a teacher for the first two years after her marriage, but now that she was a mother she settled down to become a housewife.

After Ted's birth, Ron had purchased some Christian books on marriage. One was *The Act of Marriage* by Tim and Beverly LaHaye, and another was *Total Woman* by Marabel Morgan. The content of these books was very explicit. Ron was shocked, and Joan was embarrassed and offended. The authors made clear that the explicit nature of their books was necessary for reasons of frankness and honesty. *The Act of Marriage* discussed practices that Joan felt were "gross" and "vulgar." But *Total Woman* held a special fascination for Ron. The author suggested that husbands and wives dress up and engage in all kinds of erotic antics. Joan was turned off by this; she felt that it desecrated the sanctity of the marriage bed. But Ron said that it did nothing of the kind, and encouraged Joan to be willing to experiment more. Joan complied by wearing sexy lingerie, but refused to have Ron photograph her. And she certainly would not stand for being photographed in the nude. Ron could not tell Joan that photographs of his wife in sexy lingerie or in the nude might substitute for the "skin" magazines he continued to buy occasionally.

Three years after Ted was born, Ron decided to earn his doctorate. He took Joan and the children to Wilmore, Kentucky, to live while he attended Asbury College. Once more he managed to stay away from pornographic magazines for a while. But his marital problems— which stemmed from their disagreements over dressing up and making love in exotic places and in different positions—began to take a toll on him. Their lovemaking was reduced to just once every week or two. It was a complicated but intimate matter, so neither of them wanted to tell anyone or get counseling.

After completing his doctor's degree Ron, now Dr. Barrett, was appointed by the bishop to pastor a large church in Joplin, Missouri. There the family spent five years. The problems continued, but no one knew since both Ron and Joan considered it a very private matter. After five years, Ron was appointed to his position at the Suttons' church. The Barretts met the Suttons at a reception after the 11:00 service that first Sunday. Angela and Cheryl took to each other immediately. They were destined to be the best of friends, and they saw each other almost every day. Dr. Barrett was struck by Angela's beauty, although she was only ten at the time. She was by far the most beautiful little girl Dr. Barrett had ever seen. She possessed the fairest white skin, jet black hair, rosy lips, and the loveliest blue eyes ever. She was mature-looking for her age, too. Since Angela was such a close friend of Cheryl's, Dr. Barrett was able to see her just about every day. He felt strange being attracted to a child, and she *was* a child. But there was something charming and sweet about her that Dr. Barrett could not resist. He felt somewhat guilty about his feelings for Angela, and tried to put his desire for her in the back of his mind.

After three years, something happened that paved the way for Dr. Barrett's use of Angela. On the local PBS station, the program "Masterpiece Theatre" ran a serialized version of Charles Dickens's *David Copperfield.* On the last installment, the venerable Alistair Cooke presented some details of Dickens's private life—that is, how the novel related to the author's personal life. Cooke stated that Dickens, in his middle-aged years, became infatuated with an eighteen-year-old actress and that he took her for his mistress. Dickens kept this alleged mistress of his hidden, of course, because Victorian society would not approve. He lived a double life, prim and proper on the outside but full of adultery in private. Dr. Barrett and his wife were shocked. They had never known such a thing about Dickens. But Cooke said that this was something that had been known since seven years after Dickens's death. Yet Dickens remained very popular all along. Joan was indignant. What was this old geezer talking about? she demanded, speaking of Cooke. His story is outrageous, absolutely crazy! How can such a dignified Victorian gentleman as Dickens carry on with a younger woman!? Her husband did not respond. Instead he went to an old issue of *National Geographic* which contained an article called "The England of Charles Dickens" and which provided some information on Dickens's private life. Sure enough, the article said Dickens was infatuated with a young actress named Ellen Ternan, and that his relationship with her lasted until his death in 1870. But the word "relationship" does not necessarily mean an adulterous liaison. The Barretts wondered where Alistair Cooke obtained his information. What proof did Cooke have of sexual intimacy between the staid Mr. Dickens and the lovely, youthful Miss Ternan? And why would this girl have an affair with him? To Joan it was obscene, because she had always been an admirer of Charles Dickens. But her husband thought the allegation true, as Cooke would not lie to his audience. Dr. Barrett was willing to take the word of a fatherly old gentleman like Cooke. All this information embedded itself into his brain, burying itself in his subconscious. The result was to be disastrous. Dr. Barrett formulated the idea that if a dignified, proper Victorian like Charles Dickens could live ten to twelve years of his life in private sin then why should not he, Dr. Ronald Barrett, do the same. Of course, Dr. Barrett did not think this consciously, but hid this evil thought in his subconscious.

He began his seduction of Angela slowly. He suggested to her, one day when she came over to swim in their pool, that she pose for him in her bikini. Soon he began inviting her to come over when the rest of the family was not around. He would photograph her in a bikini, or wearing the seductive lingerie he had purchased for Joan. Eventually, this led to having her pose in the nude. Dr. Barrett recalled the time Angela came over to his office in tears, saying she had had a fight with Cheryl. Cheryl's father comforted her, and during this moment of close physical contact, his desire for Angela blossomed. He had, beginning at the age of fourteen, tasted the wine of Eros and was now becoming intoxicated. He had sampled the nectar of Aphrodite, and she had snared him. He was now enslaved to her. As Ronald Barrett wiped Angela's eyes with his handkerchief, he noticed her trembling ruby lips, and he kissed them. He kissed her passionately hard, kissed her as if he could not get enough satisfaction. He picked her up and carried her over to a chair, sat her down on his lap and began caressing her. He stroked the insides of her thighs. Suddenly he stopped, telling himself he must not do this. For now, anyway, he went no further. But over the weeks, he began fondling her, progressing into foreplay. Finally, one afternoon on the first of July, he deflowered her. Of course, he felt guilt and shame, but he enjoyed the experience tremendously. He advised Angela not to tell anyone, as no one would understand.

"That wasn't all I said," Dr. Barrett was now telling Miss Marvin. "I told her it—it w-was God's will. I can't explain why I said that. I sinned. I sinned out of my own free will and choice. God had nothing to do with it. He created us humans with our own free will. What I did was against God's will." Tears came to his eyes and rolled down his cheeks. He produced a handkerchief, wiped his eyes and cheeks. "I'm sorry. I didn't mean to do this. I don't want to embarrass you. My father always said a strong man mustn't do this."

But Miss Marvin only smiled. "No one cares if you weep. Why, Jesus Himself wept. He even wept openly in public, on the way to Lazarus's tomb and on the way to Jerusalem on Palm Sunday. You know those stories, don't you?"

Dr. Barrett went on. "I tried to stop it, but I couldn't. It was like my own lust was moving me. I had become like an animal— sexually, that is. I seemed to turn into a male dog going after a female in heat. Animals have no morals, you know. But humans, being made in God's image, are supposed to be moral creatures.

"I know that God has forgiven me, but I can't forgive myself. I feel wicked and evil. What's more, I am afraid I might do it again when I leave here. Not to Angela, but maybe some other young girl who is just as beautiful."

"You should continue to receive counseling wherever you go," the therapist adjured him.

"No doubt I should."

"Tell me, did Angela ever protest about your treatment of her?"

"The second time, she objected saying that she was afraid she would become pregnant. But I solved that problem by having her use some contraceptive sponges I had originally bought for my wife. But Joan hadn't needed them in a long time, so I gave them to Angela for protection."

"Did she ever threaten to tell anyone?"

"Not until the last time I was intimate with her. When I took her home, she said she could always write a letter to the bishop. But I warned her not to tell anyone as it was our little secret as I called it."

Miss Marvin was thankful for Dr. Barrett's frankness, and she advised him to come to her at least once a week for the next few weeks.

Miss Marvin expressed a desire to meet with Joan Barrett. The discovery of her husband's infidelity with a young girl had devastated her. She had need of tranquilizers, which she was already taking, but she also needed someone to talk to. She needed professional help, from a Christian perspective. Almost all secular counselors advised their patients from a Freudian, humanistic viewpoint, and they often promoted values based on a philosophy opposed to the Judeo-Christian ethic. Joan needed spiritual counseling to set her soul at rest.

Joan sat in Miss Marvin's office explaining her dilemma to the therapist. She stated that she and Ron were currently separated because of what had happened. Miss Marvin encouraged her to tell the story about her marriage to Ron. Joan said that it might be difficult, seeing as how she felt about her spouse right now. She said that basically she was ambivalent. She felt anger, bitterness, and rage, but at the same time she felt she still loved Ron and wanted to forgive him.

Joan was a first-grade schoolteacher in Kansas City when she first met Ronald Theodore Barrett. He was the associate pastor of the church she attended. He took her out on dates to concerts, museums, parks and movies. He was never anything but gentlemanly and polite toward her. He would apologize if he even tried to kiss her after a date. He was the handsomest man she had ever met. He was to her a true-to-life "Prince Charming." He epitomized the very ideal of the man she wanted to marry. She trusted him, not only because he was a man of God but because he said he loved and respected her. They were married a year and a half after they met. Joan would never forget their wedding. She wore a gown with flowers sewn around the neck, a long white veil with more white flowers—roses— attached to her head. She remembered her best friend singing the song made popular by Elvis Presley, "Can't Help Falling in Love," which was from his movie *Blue Hawaii.* On her honeymoon, she felt no fear of having sex. She was assured that Ron would be considerate of her and not hurt her. She was free of any Victorian notions such as that no decent woman would ever enjoy it, even with her husband. Joan's mother had taught her the facts of life without putting any outmoded ideas in her head.

But after their two children were born, after they had been married for five years, Joan was aware that Ron was buying books that explained how to make one's marriage "more exciting." These books were Christian books, believe it or not. One was by Tim LaHaye and his wife, Beverly, and the other was by Marabel Morgan. Ron even had Joan read these books with him. Joan was shocked and offended by the content of these "Christian" books. The LaHaye book was not only explicit about normal practices, but described oral sex in the barest detail. And, in addition, it contained a "sex survey" of some three thousand "Christian" couples in which the respondents gave the "facts" about their sex lives. Many of the couples said that they did repulsive things to each other in order to experience sexual gratification. But the Marabel Morgan book was even worse. The author encouraged women to dress up in a provocative, erotic manner and make love in exotic places. Some of these places included under the kitchen table! Joan was revolted. It all seemed so unromantic!

But the upshot of it all was that Ron wanted her to engage in such activities as dressing up and letting him take pictures of her! Not only did he want to photograph her wearing the lingerie from Frederick's of Hollywood which he had bought for her, but he wanted to photograph her in the nude! It was too much! Joan refused, saying that it destroyed the sanctity of the marriage bed. Ron said it did no such thing and that the Bible did not forbid such antics so it was all right to engage in them. The Bible, Ron said, is really a very sexy book, especially the Song of Solomon. He would open to this passage of Scripture and quote to her the "sexy" portions. He argued that Joan was just being prudish and Victorian by not dressing up or permitting him to photograph her in the nude. Joan disputed this, saying it was not true. She was no prude! On and on this wrangling went, though they managed to keep their arguments away from the children. As preacher's kids, they had to have the best opinion of their parents.

The years went by, and nothing changed. Their love life deteriorated to the point where they made love no more than twice a month. And even then Joan did not enjoy it much. She kept praying and hoping that Ron would forget about her dressing up and such antics, but he did not. He continued to ask her to do it. Each time, however, she refused.

When they came to this church, Joan was glad to see that Cheryl had such a good friend in Angela Sutton. Angela would no doubt grow up to be a beauty, Joan had thought. She never in her born days imagined that little Angela would someday become the Other Woman.

"It has taken me a while to realize that she was a victim. I can be sorry for her, but ...." Joan burst into tears. "Sometimes I feel jealous. Yes, jealous! I tell myself not to be, but I can't help it!"

Miss Marvin handed Joan a tissue, saying, "Do you know how your daughter feels?"

"Yes," Joan sobbed, "Cheryl was angry and really upset with both Angela and Ron. But I think she has forgiven them now. It really has been a shock for me to discover that a girl my daughter was friends with turned out to be the victim of my own husband! I want to go talk to Angela, but every time I try to speak to her, she seems to draw away from me. She appears to be embarrassed. Her mother tells me that she feels full of guilt although she realizes she was victimized. She probably thinks that she has offended me."

"Try again to reach her," the therapist advised Joan. "There is no reason for her to feel guilty. She was a victim. I have already told her that several times."

Joan said that she would try, but it would indeed be difficult.

❄

April had turned into May, and the lilac blossoms "rusted," the tulips gave way to peonies and lilies-of-the-valley. The days grew warmer and things began to improve for both the Suttons and the Barretts. Angela was doing better in school, thanks largely to her counseling. Her parents were more attentive to her personal needs. Florence quit her job and went to work telecommuting from home so she could spend more time with her daughter. And Mark began to show more affection for Angela. He bought a blond male cocker spaniel puppy for her. Angela was delighted, and she named the pup Franklin after President Franklin Pierce.

VIII

On Mother's Day, Dr. Barrett asked his wife to meet him in the park across the street from the church building. Joan wondered what the meeting was about, as she had not seen her husband since that last evening when he had shown up at the parsonage and related to her his plans for the future.

Joan sat on a bench waiting for Ron to appear. She was growing apprehensive wondering what he had to say to her. At last she saw him approaching. She invited him to sit next to her on the park bench.

"Why did you want to see me, Ron?" she queried. "I've been on pins and needles all this time."

"I want to speak to you about us," he replied. "Joan, I want you and the kids with me when I move away to my new job."

"I suppose I'll go with you. But it won't be the same. Nothing will ever be the same between us ever again. You know that, Ronald."

"I know and I understand. Don't think I don't."

"Why, Ron, why did you do it? I'm talking about Angela now. Why did you do what you did?"

"What can I say? I was motivated by my own desire. You know what the Bible says about lust. Every person is tempted by his own lust. And if he yields, he sins. When I first saw Angela Sutton, four years ago, I was drawn to her sexually—despite her age. I never thought someone so young could be so appealing, but she was. I started having fantasies about her although they were generally unbidden at first. When she began to grow up, I started to look at her more. And then I began photographing her. All the rest you know. I acted compulsively, like I had lost my own free agency. I don't know what came over me. I knew very well it was wrong, but I acted anyway. I suppose those magazines you found influenced my behavior, however I mustn't lay all the blame there."

"Angela told me that you said to her one time that it was God's will that you should do what you did. How can you say such a thing? As a minister, you know that what you did was sin and that God doesn't cause sin to happen. You know you acted out of your own free will. Why did you tell Angela that it was God's will?"

"I don't know."

"Oh, come now, Ronald Barrett, you know I can't accept that as an answer. You can come up with something better than that, can't you?"

"No, I really can't. Except to say that apparently Satan put it into my mind to tell Angela that."

"Oh, so now you're going to blame it all on the Devil. Don't give me that Flip Wilson excuse. You acted irresponsibly."

"No, I don't mean that to be an excuse. I know perfectly well it was my fault and no one else's. But I just want to say that the Evil One can put ideas in a person's mind. The pornography I was buying and keeping hidden, and the things I saw on TV can all play a part in what a person thinks. As a person thinks in his heart so is he."

They sat silently together for a few moments, thinking of happier times. Suddenly Joan broke into tears. Ron folded his arms around her to comfort her.

"I'm sorry, Joan. How many times can I say that?"

Joan straightened up, wiping her eyes. "I don't know, Ron. I want to forget and forgive you. But it is the forgetting, not the forgiving, that is going to be difficult. How can we go on living as man and wife, remembering what came between us? Every time you would take me in your arms, I'll think of Angela. Even now I get mental images—unbidden, of course—of you and her together, and it just...." She began to cry again.

Ron took her tissue in his hand and wiped her eyes for her. She seemed like a helpless and hurt child. His conscience assailed him again. "Look, Joan, if you don't think it will work, then we can end it all."

"You mean a divorce? No, Ron, think of the children. Think what our divorcing would do to them. It would tear their lives apart. We will have to just try to work it out somehow. Maybe I can try to forget." She stood up in order to leave.

"Wait, Joan," Ron stopped her. "It starts in the heart. It starts with forgiveness. As ones who follow Christ, shouldn't we be forgiving one another as God in Christ has forgiven us? Don't say that forgiveness and reconciliation are impossible. With God nothing is impossible. We have been receiving counseling, and I know that although I have a problem, we can work it out."

"I'll try, dear," Joan responded. And, with calling him that affectionate term, Joan was on her way to reconciliation with her spouse.

"Before you go, Joanie," Ron stopped her again, "I have something for you." From inside his jacket pocket Ron pulled out a card in a pink envelope. "Happy Mother's Day, sweetheart."

Joan accepted the card, smiling, with tears of joy filling her eyes.

❊

The weeks went by, and it was now June. The Suttons' garden was abloom with red, white and pink roses. The days were now turning hot, and soon summer would be arriving.

Angela arrived at her counseling session with Miss Marvin the first Friday of the month. Miss Marvin commented on the improvement in Angela since she first started coming to Our Healer Counseling Center. The girl was no longer as depressed and withdrawn as she had been.

"There are some people here to see you, Angela," the therapist said as she took her patient back to the counseling room.

"Who?" Angela inquired.

"Wait 'til you see."

Miss Marvin opened the door, and as Angela walked in she saw that Dr. and Mrs. Barrett were waiting for her. Immediately she shied up. She had not seen Dr. Barrett since the Sunday before she began therapy, and now she was afraid to talk to him. She had been deliberately avoiding him as she felt her getting well depended on such avoidance.

Angela returned Mrs. Barrett's greeting politely, but when Dr. Barrett said "Good morning, Angela," to her, she murmured a response in a low voice. She was not trying to be rude, but she was embarrassed.

"I brought the Barretts here to meet with you," stated Miss Marvin, "because, for one reason, they are leaving for Pennsylvania tomorrow. Also, I believe Dr. Barrett has something to tell you."

Angela sat down on a sofa while Dr. Barrett stood across the room by the window. She still could not look at him.

"Have you been doing well, Angela?" Dr. Barrett asked.

"Um, yes, sir," Angela replied.

"You need not feel embarrassed, Angel. My wife and I have been receiving therapy here, too. You see, I have a problem. Part of what contributed to my doing what I did is my addiction to a certain type of magazine. It is the kind of magazine which exploits women, showing them in the nude and semi-nude. I can't help but want to look at such pictures. That is what led me to photographing you posed in the same ways. I then misused you. I took advantage of your innocence, youth, and trust. I also took advantage of your respect for my position of authority. I'm sorry."

He approached the sofa where Angela was seated. He sat down beside her, reaching out to touch her hand. She recoiled from his touch as if afraid of him.

"It's all right, Angel. I just want to tell you something. I take full responsibility for what happened. None of it was your fault. It was all my doing. You need not feel conscience-stricken, Angel."

Angela spoke to him directly, looking him straight in the eye. "Please, Dr. Barrett, I wish you wouldn't call me that. My name is Angela. The nickname 'Angel' sounds like a contradiction in terms. I felt guilty because I always thought I could say no, but I didn't. I am beginning to understand what you are telling me. I only recently realized that I was victimized by you, and that I am not a bimbo."

"I did not intend to make you feel that way about yourself, Angela," Dr. Barrett said. "It's just my appreciation of natural beauty and my erotic addiction that propelled me to act the way I did. It's an addiction sort of like alcoholism. You know, when a person wants to stop drinking, but he can't. Well, there is such a thing as sexual addiction. That is what I have. I am going to have to continue getting treatment for it no matter where I live."

"I understand now," Angela said. "And, Dr. Barrett, you don't have to feel guilty and ashamed anymore. God has forgiven you, and I forgive you."

She embraced both Dr. and Mrs. Barrett before they commenced talking more about the place where the Barretts were going to live. Angela kept saying how much she was going to miss Cheryl and Ted. Mrs. Barrett assured Angela that she could write them whenever she wished. She wrote down the new mailing address of her family so that Angela could write them.

The next day, Saturday, as the Barretts were getting ready to leave, Angela went over to the parsonage to say goodbye. She gave them each a hug, saying she would write. When she came to Cheryl, they discussed old times together—like the time the third-grade class sang "Puff, the Magic Dragon," in the school pageant, and making "snowpeople" in new-fallen snow. Most memorable of all were the camping trips they had gone on together and the bird-watching expeditions.

"I sure will miss you, Angela," Cheryl said, tears coming to her eyes. "I am truly sorry that I was ever mad at you. You know, about the thing with Dad. I did not understand at first, but now I do."

Angela hugged Cheryl again. "You're forgiven, Cheryl. I didn't understand it myself at first. I felt guilty and dirty. But now I believe everything is going to be all right."

They all said farewell again, and then the Barretts left. Angela stood waving until their van was out of sight. She blinked to keep the tears from falling, knowing that she was definitely going to miss her great friend.

❄

The months went by. Angela made friends with the new senior pastor and his wife. Dr. Marlin Smothers and Gwendolyn Smothers were middle-aged, about the same age as Angela's parents. They had two sons and two daughters who were grown up and living away from them. Angela was not disappointed to learn that they did not have a daughter her own age since she had so many friends her age. One person who was not Angela's age but was still her friend was Mrs. Keller. The two of them became friendly all over again, and it was as if nothing had ever happened to cause Mrs. Keller to disapprove of Angela.

One evening in October, Angela was babysitting for Travis Clark at his home. She enjoyed babysitting, reading to the little tykes and playing games with them. Soon it came time to put Travis to bed.

"Do I have to go, Angela?" whined Travis.

"Oh, yes, you need your sleep, Travis. I tell you what—I'll sing you a song after I tuck you in. OK?"

"OK."

Travis went off to get ready for bed while Angela pondered what she was going to sing to him. When she came in to Travis's room and tucked him into bed, she asked the little boy what song he would like her to sing to him.

"How about that one we sang in church last Sunday. You know, the one about loving Jesus," suggested Travis.

"You mean, 'My Jesus I Love Thee'?" asked Angela.

"Yeah, that's the one. I think."

Angela began singing her favorite hymn to the child. Suddenly, there flashed into her mind the memory of the many times this hymn had been sung in church when Dr. Barrett was there. The memory of seeing him singing this song filled her thoughts, and she almost stopped singing. Pain struck her heart.

"What's the matter, Angela?" asked Travis. "Why aren't you singing so loud anymore?"

"Oh, nothing." Angela tried to put the past out of her mind. Just then she remembered that believers should forgive each other their trespasses. And she also recalled that forgiveness meant not only not holding a grudge, but also not dwelling on memories of past wrongs. She finished her song to Travis and, with each word, the pain in her soul and spirit faded away. She knew that God uses the Christian's bad experiences for good. That was one of His greatest miracles: bringing good out of human evil and wrongdoing. What was more, this seemingly negative experience could change her, Angela Miriam Sutton, for the better. There was a lilt to her singing voice as she rose out of the pits of grief to the heights of joy in her Savior.